The Plant Based Air Fryer Cookbook

The Ultimate Vegan Air Fryer Recipe Book. With Over 100 Healthy, Delicious and Whole Food Vegan Recipes for Easy and Successful Weight Loss. 21 Day Meal Plan Included.

Monica Fisher

Legal Notice:

Copyright 2023 by Monica Fisher- All rights reserved.

Disclaimer Notice:

Table of Contents

INTRODUCTION 7

   BASICS OF AIR FRYER COOKING.................................... 7

BENEFITS OF A PLANT-BASED DIET...................... 10

5 TIPS AND TRICKS 11

COMMON MISTAKES.. 13

BREAKFAST AND BRUNCH RECIPES 14

   1.   PLANT BASED FRENCH TOAST..15

   2.   TOFU SCRAMBLE 16

   3.   BLUEBERRY PANCAKE...17

   4.   AIR FRYER PLANT BASED POTATO PANCAKES 18

   5.   AIR FRYER BRUSCHETTA...19

   6.   AIR FRYER VEGAN QUICHE 20

   7.   VEGAN FRITTATA 21

   8.   VEGAN AIR FRIED MAC AND CHEESE 22

   9.   AIR FRYER VEGAN TOFU SANDWICHES 23

   10.   VEGAN BREAKFAST POTATO HASH 24

   11. VEGAN CINNAMON OATMEAL 25

   12.   VEGAN POLENTA... 26

   13.   SUGAR FREE AIR FRYER COCOA PUDDING 27

   14.   VEGAN AIR FRYER GRANOLA 28

   15. SUGAR FREE QUINOA BREAKFAST 29

   16.   POTATOES AND COCONUT CREAM BOWL 30

   17. BREAKFAST BURRITOS..31

   18.   LEEK AND MUSHROOM OMELET 32

   19. CHICKPEAS AND SHALLOTS BOWL 33

20.   PUMPKIN OATMEAL 34

VEGAN PLANT BASED AIR FRYER APPETIZERS...............................**35**

21.   VEGAN AIR FRYER HUSH PUPPIES 36
22.   AIR FRYER BEETS 37
23.   AIR FRYER POTATO WEDGES 38
24.   AVOCADO ROLLS 39
25.   WHOLE VEGAN AIR FRYER SAMOSA 40
26.   KALE AND POTATO NUGGETS 41
27.   VEGAN CHICKPEA MEATBALLS 42
28.   AIR FRYER ACORN SQUASH 43
29.   AIR FRYER VEGAN CALAMARI 44
30.   POTATO PATTIES 45
31.   AIR FRYER PLANTAINS 46
32.   LENTIL MEATBALLS 47
33.   SPICY BANANA CHIPS 48
34.   CHICKPEA FALAFEL 49
35.   CABBAGE FRITTERS 50
36.   CAULIFLOWER WINGS 51
37.   ROASTED BRUSSELS SPROUTS 52
38.   ZUCCHINI CORN FRITTERS 53
39.   SMOKEY CHICKPEAS 54
40.   KALE CHIPS 55

PLANT BASED VEGAN AIR FRYER MAIN RECIPES **56**

41.   EGGPLANT VEGAN PASTA 57
42.   AIR FRYER VEGAN BEAN BURGERS 59
43.   AIR FRYER VEGAN QUORN VEGAN FILLETS WITH RICE 60
44.   VEGAN PLANT BASED FAJITAS 61
45.   PLANT BASED VEGAN PULLED PORK 62
46.   AIR FRYER TOFU VEGGIE STIR FRY 63
47.   VEGAN CAULIFLOWER TACOS 64
48.   VEGAN AIR FRYER MUSHROOM BURGERS 65
49.   PLANT BASED VEGAN AIR FRYER RATATOUILLE 66

50.   VEGAN RICE BALLS WITH SAUCE 67

51. VEGAN POTATO CURRY 68

52. VEGAN BULGUR STEAKS 69

53. VEGAN TORTILLAS 70

54. VEGAN AIR FRYER PASTA 72

55. VEGAN CAULIFLOWER WITH HARISSA SAUCE 73

56. VEGAN POTATOES AND CHICKPEAS 74

57. VEGAN CHICKPEA BURGERS 75

58. VEGAN TOFU TACOS 76

59. VEGAN ZUCCHINI GRATIN 78

60. VEGAN CAULIFLOWER SAUTÉ 79

AIR FRYER WHOLE VEGAN SIDES AND SALADS 80

61. VEGAN SPICY TOFU SALAD 81

62. WHOLE VEGAN SWEET POTATO ROLLS 82

63. VEGAN AIR FRYER CRUNCHY SALAD 83

64. VEGAN AIR FRYER SPINACH SALAD 84

65. VEGAN AIR FRYER EGGPLANT SALAD 85

66. VEGAN AIR FRYER TOFU VERMICELLI SALAD 86

67. VEGAN AIR FRYER TOMATO CAPRESE SALAD 87

68. VEGAN AIR FRYER BUTTON MUSHROOM SALAD 88

69. VEGAN AIR FRYER GREEN BEAN SALAD 89

70. VEGAN AIR FRYER LETTUCE AND CORN SALAD 90

VEGAN AIR FRYER SNACKS 91

71. VEGAN AIR FRYER TOFU 92

72. VEGAN AIR FRYER ZUCCHINI CHIPS 93

73. VEGAN AIR FRYER POTATO FRIES 94

74. VEGAN AIR FRYER CABBAGE CHIPS 95

75. VEGAN AIR FRYER OKRA 96

76. VEGAN AIR FRYER ONION RINGS 97

77. VEGAN AIR FRYER AVOCADO FRIES 98

78. VEGAN AIR FRYER GARLICKY POTATO NUGGETS 99

79. VEGAN AIR FRYER CARROTS FRIES 100

80. VEGAN AIR FRYER CASSAVA ROOT FRIES 101

81. VEGAN AIR FRYER QUINOA STUFFED PEPPERS 102

82. VEGAN AIR FRYER VEGAN PIZZA 103

83. VEGAN AIR FRYER ROSTI 104

84. VEGAN AIR FRYER BEET CHIPS 105

85. VEGAN AIR FRYER CASHEWS 106

WHOLE VEGAN AIR FRYER DESSERT RECIPES 107

86. VEGAN AIR FRYER APRICOT PIE 108

87. VEGAN AIR FRYER SUGAR-FREE VEGAN BROWNIES 109

88. VEGAN AIR FRYER SUGAR-FREE VEGAN WALNUT MUFFINS 110

89. VEGAN AIR FRIED PEACHES 111

90. BANANA CAKE 112

91. VEGAN AIR FRIED OREO.. 113

92. VEGAN AIR FRIED DONUTS 114

93. VEGAN AIR FRIED COOKIES 115

94. VEGAN AIR FRIED CARROT CAKE 116

95. VEGAN AIR FRIED ALMOND BICUITS 117

96. VEGAN AIR FRIED CANNOLI 118

97. VEGAN AIR FRIED ORANGE CAKE 119

98. VEGAN AIR FRIED CHOCOLATE DIPPED DONUTS 120

99. VEGAN AIR FRIED PUDDING..122

100. VEGAN AIR FRIED MONKEY BREAD 123

101. VEGAN AIR FRIED VEGAN MACAROONS..124

THANKS FOR READING 129

Introduction

The air fryer has gained popularity over the past ten to fifteen years due to its ease of use and as a healthier form of cooking favorite foods that would typically be deep fried. That said, the air fryer can do much more than just fry food. Depending on the type and size you have chosen, air fryers can bake, roast, broil, crisp, dehydrate, and reheat foods of many different types. In addition, the air fryer provides a lower-fat method of cooking that can preserve nutrients in foods at higher levels than many other forms of cooking. This is especially important if you are focused on a plant-based diet.

This cookbook is about using the air fryer to enhance and diversify your options on a plant-based diet. Each recipe can be created with the air fryer in whole or part. This creates a meal with less effort and allows for more time spent doing other things.

Basics of Air Fryer Cooking

The air fryer is a highly versatile countertop appliance that is quickly becoming a staple in many homes. The air fryer does come in different styles and versions to meet the needs of your family size and meal needs. The three main versions are a single basket, a double basket, and the toaster oven style. All are small enough to be kept on the counter in your kitchen and offer various cooking options. The single basket is best for those who are single or a couple. The double basket is best for families of 3-4, though they can also be used to cook multiple items at the same time at different temperatures. Finally, the convection oven air fryer type can be used to create larger amounts of food for larger families or can replace a typical oven in some instances.

While using an air fryer is pretty intuitive, there are a few basics that users should be aware of when using the appliance. First, know that some people put off getting an air fryer because a slow cooker or Instant Pot seemed to be enough, but for those who delve into the air frying world, the ability to create quick, delicious, healthy meals is the best part of air fryer ownership. The basket-type air fryers are the most popular, though the convection oven type may be more versatile and better for larger meals. The best part of the dual basket-type air fryer is the ability to cook two separate items in the baskets at different times and temperatures. Using only the air fryer can quickly create a main component and side dish. The air fryer is also a bonus when it is hot outside, and cooking in an oven makes the house too warm.

Almost anything can be cooked in an air fryer, including plant-based food options. For example, vegetables can be air fried, baked, or heated in the air fryer easily, and little to no oil is necessary. The only thing you must remember when using the air fryer is not to overcrowd the basket and not to use ingredients that are too wet placed directly in the basket. Since the air fryer works by having a heating element that radiates heat and a fan to circulate hot air around the basket to cook food, you need space. This hot air circulation allows for less oil than traditional frying while still creating the texture and crispiness that people desire. The air fryer can also brown and caramelize nicely to create delicious flavor on vegetables, proteins, and more.

If you are a new air fryer user, then make sure to read the manual well, but to get started, there are a few safety tips that should be practiced.

- The air fryer is for air frying, not oil frying. Therefore, the basket should never be filled with oil.
- Make sure your air fryer is well-ventilated and not pushed up against a wall because it can overheat. The air fryer needs to ventilate the exhaust for safety and even cooking.
- Any food with a low smoke point, like bacon, should be cooked at a temperature slightly lower than normal to prevent burning from the grease that is produced. The same applies to oils that should not be overheated because this could lead to spattering or burns.
- When food is done cooking, the air fryer basket will be hot. Do not sit it directly on a countertop or table; protect surfaces with a trivet or hot pad. Be careful not to touch the hot basket with your bare hand as you may be burned.
- When the air fryer is not in use, unplug it. Do not sit the air fryer on the stove even when in use. These are just safety issues that are common to most small appliances.

When you are ready to try out your first meal of side in the air fryer, there are also some key tips and tricks to remember to make sure your meal turns out as you expect.

- Most importantly, do not crowd the basket. The air needs room to circulate for foods to get crispy and cooked. Therefore, unless a recipe calls for it, food should be in a single layer in the air fryer basket. This can mean multiple batches for larger quantities of some foods.
- Choose the proper temperature. While most recipes give you the temperature that is ideal for cooking, if creating your own version of a dish, then it can be confusing. As a rule of thumb, think about what you would set the oven on for the dish, lower it by 25 degrees, and this is the proper air fryer temperature.
- Feel free to check the basket. When using the air fryer, it does not hurt the process to open the basket and check on your food. In fact, when cooking small pieces of food or something that needs to be cooked from both sides, open and shake the basket slightly to allow for even cooking on all sides. If cooking meat, flip each piece midway through the cooking time.
- Utilize presets. Most air fryers have several preset programs for common foods. These are great for beginners, but as you become familiar with the air fryer, feel free to set your own time and temperature for the cooking style you prefer.
- Drier foods get crispier. Almost any food type can be used in the air fryer, but the dryer a piece of food, the crispier it will get. For example, before breading vegetables, dry the cleaned pieces as much as possible with a paper towel, then bread. Even moist foods will cook, but crispier foods require a drier start.
- Preheat the air fryer. Preheating is just to allow for the most even cooking. To preheat your air fryer, turn it to the desired temperature for about 5 minutes before placing food in the basket. If you choose not to preheat, allow a few extra minutes of cooking time for your food.

- Air fryers can be used for reheating and crisping foods back up as leftovers. When reheating, set the temperature about 30 degrees lower than the temperature you would cook it at in the air fryer.

Making a tasty meal in less time and with less effort is wonderful. The air fryer not only makes cooking easier, but cleanup is also straightforward. Most air fryers have a nonstick coating making the cleanup simple. For most basket-style types, an inner and outer basket can be separated and then cleaned with warm, soapy water. Dry both components well before placing them back into the appliance. Use a soft cloth on all air fryer components to avoid damaging the pieces. This includes wiping down the outside when it is dirty. Depending on the brand, some air fryer components may be dishwasher safe, but repeated cleanings in the dishwasher can be tough on the components over time. The oven-style air fryer parts that are removable can be cleaned with warm, soapy water as well and should be dried before replacing. If desired, you can use parchment paper or foil inside the air fryer to keep it cleaner. However, never turn the appliance on with paper or foil in the basket or on the tray if there is not also food. The parchment paper or foil can touch the heating element and cause issues.

Benefits of a Plant-Based Diet

Plant-based diets are not new. Many people have chosen a vegan or vegetarian lifestyle for different reasons, but what are the actual benefits of this type of diet? There are plenty of benefits to eating a plant-based diet that goes beyond the political or humanitarian reasons many people choose to avoid meat. Research shows that plant-based diets can serve as low-risk and cost-effective interventions to reduce cancer risks, lower blood pressure, lower body mass index, and improve cholesterol levels. Furthermore, plant-based diets can be beneficial to those with chronic disease in conjunction with necessary medications. Plant-based diets can reduce the need for healthcare because you are healthier or reduce the number of medications needed for chronic disorders. Both of these represent improved or better health for an individual. Some chronic diseases can drastically improve with a plant-based diet.

Diet fads come and go, but a plant-based diet has been around for a couple of decades as a way to reduce health problems and live a healthier lifestyle. A plant-based diet is not necessarily the same as a vegan or vegetarian lifestyle because the meat is allowed but within limits. Basically, a plant-based diet is eating mostly plants like whole grains, vegetables, and fruits for each meal. Two-thirds of your plate for each meal should be plant-based options, with the remaining third being a lean protein or a plant protein like beans or tofu. Choosing a plant-based diet means you can eat fruits and vegetables that are in season, eat cheaper, and still have a wide variety of food options.

Plant-based diets support the immune system with vitamins and minerals not found in other foods. The vitamins and minerals keep your body in balance with healthy cells that boost the immune system. Additionally, plant-based diets can help eliminate inflammation in the body to help keep you feeling your best. Long-term inflammation in the body can cause damage and lead to diseases like cancer and arthritis. While a plant-based diet does not guarantee that you will never get sick, it does offer a better chance of avoiding some common issues.

Plant-based diets can also help you to maintain a healthy weight or cause a reduction in weight if you are carrying a few extra pounds. This is partly due to the extra fiber that will be present, which will help with digestion and elimination within the body. All that said, a plant-based diet is only beneficial if you prepare the meals in a healthy way. For example, deep-fried vegetables are unhealthy, but air-fried vegetables can be healthier. Avoid overly processed foods like crackers or cookies; even the healthy version of these options is best left at the store. Pastas and rice are fine within reason, but whole-grain or brown versions are best. Preparing these in the proper way can create healthy, flavor-filled meals that anyone can enjoy. Above all, make the transition slowly, introducing more plant-based options into your life over time so the change is easier to maintain. Suddenly choosing plant-based diets can lead to failure if the eater is not used to these types of foods.

5 Tips and Tricks

Making changes to your lifestyle or changing how your family eats and prepares meals can be tough, but we have some tips and tricks to help you make a gradual transition to using the air fryer and consuming a plant-based diet. Below are the five best tips and tricks for making these healthy changes.

Start Slow – Change is tough. Whether you are cooking just for yourself or an entire family, make changes slowly. It will take you time to get used to using the air fryer and switching to a plant-based diet. Start experimenting with a few simple recipes at a time as sides or a main dish paired with other favorites. For example, try serving air-fried chicken with some air-fried veggies as a side for practice with your air fryer and a healthy meal. Try adding one to two meals each week for a month that are plant-based and air-fried as you make the transition.

Have Fun – Turn meals into family time or a fun event with friends. Food is the center of so much in different cultures. Experiment with plant-based options and the air fryer to create meals everyone can enjoy. Allow children to help prepare meals, shop for ingredients, and serve so they feel like part of the process. Consider having an air fryer party where everyone brings their favorite air-fried dish to share with others. Changes in the way you prepare food or the foods you eat can be tricky, but having friends and family to support the changes is helpful. Learn to see cooking and food choices as an interesting and diverse part of life instead of a chore to help make changes easier. You can also prepare snacks and ingredients ahead of time to save precious minutes on busy days. Have veggie snack options like carrots, cut fruit, hummus, and salsa ready to go before the week starts. We tend to choose foods based on convenience.

Build Your Base – Keep in mind that a plant-based diet is not about being a vegetarian or vegan, though you have this option. The trick is to start with your base and build from there. Start with a salad of fresh greens, tomatoes, peppers, and other favorite salad ingredients, and then add some chicken pieces from the air fryer as a protein. This is still plant-based because the meal is predominantly plant and vegetable, with a small amount being lean meat. For children, add a bit of cheese or a drizzle of dressing to encourage eating. Try to add color to the dish with yellow bell peppers, bright red tomatoes, cucumbers, and other colorful options for appeal. You can even end this meal with a fruit-based dessert that is sweet yet healthy. Many simple desserts can be prepared in the air fryer as you enjoy your meal.

Pre Plan – Planning a menu ahead of time, a week, two weeks, or even a month in advance, can be helpful when starting a new diet. Fresh fruits and vegetables are always best on a plant-based diet, so plan a menu based on what is in season and available in your area. This can save money because the ingredients are plentiful at the time. Shop farmer's markets and roadside stands for deals on foods that will keep for a week or two so you can have ingredients on hand and ready to go as needed. Knowing what you are having for each meal can save time and effort in trying to make a decision and ultimately choosing something unhealthy. Planning a menu at first can feel overwhelming, but with practice, it will become second nature. Allow your family to help with the planning to make meal times easier.

Cheat Day – A plant-based diet is a lifestyle, not something short-term. The plant-based options are about eating healthier without being overly limiting. When first starting your plant-based diet, give yourself one day a week to eat something fun and fattening. Enjoy a bowl of ice cream or a couple of doughnuts on occasion. The goal is not to deny yourself but to make healthy changes to the point that you naturally start choosing healthier options. Too often, people fail at lifestyle changes because they are too strict with themselves. We all need a treat on occasion. Whether focused on air frying, plant-based meals, or both, take a break occasionally so you do not get overwhelmed with changes or bored with a lack of variety.

Common Mistakes

Change is tough. We are creatures of habit, even when those habits may be unhealthy or create more problems. Below are some of the most common mistakes in switching to air-fried foods and a plant-based diet.

Boredom – Not every meal has to be totally air fried, nor do only green vegetables need to be used. Variety is important when it comes to making dietary changes. Add some variety to your meals, whether changing for yourself or as a family. For example, try a vegetarian lasagna one night, create salads with lots of colors, and encourage your children to pick a new fruit or vegetable to try each week. Ensure you add flavor to your dishes with spices that can take food to new levels.

Overcooking – The air fryer cooks differently than your oven. Practice with different settings and temperatures to determine what produces the food you love. For example, some people prefer vegetables cooked a bit crispier than others and may cook for a few minutes longer. The air fryer is like any other appliance; you must practice with it to get the results you desire. Embrace the learning experience.

Foods Too Wet – The air fryer can cook many types of food, but those in a super wet batter or foods with a high moisture content may not do as well. If using freshly washed vegetables, make sure to pat them dry gently with a clean towel or paper towel before air frying for the best results.

Overfilling – It can be tempting to fill the air fryer basket to the brim with fries, veggies, or other foods, but the air must be able to circulate to cook foods properly. Make sure foods have room to cook, even if you must cook multiple batches. The air fryer is faster than a traditional fryer or oven, so even multiple batches can be cooked rapidly.

Working with a new appliance or considering a new plant-based diet can feel overwhelming. Still, the health benefits paired with the wonderful dishes created in this cookbook will have you embracing the changes quickly and without looking back. So, let's get started on some interesting dishes that will make you feeling great.

Breakfast and Brunch Recipes

1. PLANT BASED FRENCH TOAST

Servings|4 Time|7 minutes

Nutritional Content (per serving):

Cal |180Fat |9g Protein |7g Carbs| 20g Fibre| 2g

Ingredients:

- 4 slices of sugar-free vegan bread (such as whole grain or sprouted grain)
- 250 ml (1 cup) of unsweetened almond milk

- 30 grams (2 tablespoons) of cornstarch
- 16 grams (2 teaspoons) of sugar substitute (such as stevia or erythritol)
- 8 grams (1 teaspoon) of vanilla extract
- 2 grams (1/4 teaspoon) of cinnamon
- 2 grams (1/4 teaspoon) of salt
- 50 grams (1/4 cup) of vegan buttery spread
- 60 ml (¼ cup) of sugar-free syrup and fresh fruit for serving (optional)

Directions:

1. In a large bowl, whisk together the plant-based milk, cornstarch, sugar substitute, vanilla extract, cinnamon, and salt until well combined.
2. Dip each slice of bread into the mixture, making sure to fully coat both sides.
3. In a separate bowl, melt the vegan buttery spread.
4. Dip each slice of bread into the melted buttery spread and place it in the air fryer basket. Repeat with the remaining slices.
5. Set the air fryer to 200°C (400°F) and cook the French toast for 6-7 minutes, or until golden brown.
6. Serve hot with sugar-free syrup and fresh fruit, if desired. Enjoy!

> **Note:**

This recipe provides a delicious and healthier alternative to traditional French toast, as it eliminates the use of sugar and dairy and uses a healthier cooking method. The air fryer also creates a crispy exterior that is perfect for soaking up syrup and other toppings. Enjoy!

2. TOFU SCRAMBLE

Servings|2 Time|25 minutes

Nutritional Content (per serving):

Cal |125Fat |8g Protein |12g Carbs| 13g Fibre| 1.8g

Ingredients:

- ❖ 1 block of drained and crumbled extra firm tofu
- ❖ 15 ml (1 tablespoon) of olive or avocado oil
- ❖ 1/2 a yellow onion, finely diced
- ❖ 1 red bell pepper, diced
- ❖ 2 cloves of garlic, minced

- ❖ 8 grams (1 teaspoon) of turmeric
- ❖ 4 grams (1/2 teaspoon) of cumin
- ❖ 4 grams (1/2 teaspoon) of chili powder
- ❖ 1 grain (1 pinch) of salt and pepper, to taste
- ❖ 30 grams (2 tablespoons) of nutritional yeast
- ❖ 8 grams (1 teaspoon) of sugar-free sweetener, such as stevia or erythritol
- ❖ Fresh herbs like parsley or cilantro for garnish (optional)

Directions:

1. Preheat your air fryer to 200°C (400° F).
2. In a large mixing bowl, combine the crumbled tofu, turmeric, cumin, chili powder, salt, pepper, nutritional yeast, and sugar-free sweetener. Stir until everything is well combined.
3. Now heat the avocado oil in a large deep skillet over a medium heat. Add the diced onion, red bell pepper, and minced garlic, and cook until the onion is translucent, about 5 minutes.
4. Add the tofu mixture to the skillet and cook for an additional 5-7 minutes, stirring occasionally.
5. Transfer the tofu scramble to a heat-proof dish that will fit in the air fryer.
6. Cook the tofu scramble in the air fryer for 10-12 minutes, or until it is heated through and crispy on top.
7. Serve the tofu scrambled hot, garnished with fresh herbs if desired. Enjoy!

3. BLUEBERRY PANCAKE

Servings|4 Time|10 minutes

Nutritional Content (per serving):

Cal |235Fat |11.3g Protein |7.5g Carbs| 16.8g Fibre| 2g

Ingredients:

- ❖ 125 grams (1 cup) of fall-purpose
- ❖ 15 grams (2 teaspoons) baking powder
- ❖ 2 gram (1/4 teaspoon) of salt
- ❖ 60 ml (1/4 cup) of unsweetened plant-based milk (such as almond, soy, or oat milk)

- ❖ 15 ml (1 tablespoon) of lemon juice
- ❖ 15ml (1 tablespoon) of melted vegan butter or coconut oil
- ❖ 5ml (1 teaspoon) of vanilla extract
- ❖ 200 grams (1 cup) of fresh or frozen blueberries

Directions:

1. In a large bowl, whisk together the flour, baking powder, and salt.
2. In a separate bowl, mix the plant-based milk with the lemon juice and let sit for a few minutes to curdle and create a "buttermilk" effect.
3. Add the melted vegan butter or coconut oil, and vanilla extract to the "buttermilk" and whisk to combine.
4. Now, pour your wet mixture into the prepared dry mixture and stir very well until everything is very well combined.
5. Gently add in the blueberries.
6. Preheat your air fryer to 180°C (360°F).
7. Spoon about 1/4 cup of the batter into the air fryer basket for each pancake.
8. Cook the pancakes for about 8-10 minutes or until lightly golden brown, flipping halfway through.
9. Serve hot with your favorite toppings.
10. Enjoy your delicious, sugar-free, plant-based, blueberry pancakes made in the air fryer!

4. AIR FRYER PLANT BASED POTATO PANCAKES

Servings|4 Time|15 minutes

Nutritional Content (per serving):

Cal |201Fat |8.9g Protein |10g   Carbs| 14.3g Fibre| 2.1g

Ingredients:

- 2 large russet potatoes, grated 250 grams (½ pound)
- 1/2 onion, finely grated
- 1 grain (1 pinch) of sea salt
- 1 grain (1 pinch) of sea salt
- 2 tablespoons (30 grams) of all-purpose flour or also you can use gluten-free flour
- 2 tablespoons of melted coconut oil

Directions:

1. In a large bowl, mix the grated potatoes, onion, salt, pepper, and flour.
2. Add in the melted coconut oil to your ingredients.
3. Preheat your air fryer to a temperature of about 200°C (400°F).
4. Scoop 2 tablespoons of the potato mixture into your hand and press it into a thick pancake.
5. Repeat this process until you have used up all the mixture, making about 8-10 pancakes.
6. Place the pancakes in the air fryer basket, making sure not to overcrowd it.
7. Cook the pancakes for 10-12 minutes, flipping halfway through, or until they are golden brown and crispy.
8. Serve hot with your favorite dipping sauce.
9. Enjoy your delicious, sugar-free, plant-based potato pancakes made in the air fryer!

5. AIR FRYER BRUSCHETTA

Servings|2-3 Time|6 minutes

Nutritional Content (per serving):

Cal |153Fat |13g Protein |8g   Carbs| 13g Fibre| 2 g

Ingredients:

- 4 ripe tomatoes, diced
- 40 grams (¼ cup) of chopped fresh basil
- 2 cloves of garlic, minced
- 15 ml (1 tablespoon) of olive oil
- 4 grams (1/2 teaspoon) of salt
- 2 grams (1/4 teaspoon) of ground black pepper

- 8 slices of a baguette or other crusty bread
- 30 ml (2 tablespoon) of melted coconut oil
- 40 grams (1/4cup) Vegan parmesan cheese (optional)

Directions:

1. In a large bowl, mix the diced tomatoes, basil, garlic, olive oil, salt, and pepper.
2. Start by preheating your air fryer to a temperature of about 200°C (400°F).
3. Brush both sides of the bread slices with the melted vegan butter or coconut oil.
4. Place the bread slices in the air fryer basket, making sure not to overcrowd it.
5. Cook the bread for 2-3 minutes or until toasted and crispy.
6. Generously put one spoon of tomato mixture onto each slice of bread.
7. Return the bruschetta to the air fryer basket and cook for an additional 2-3 minutes or until the tomato mixture is heated through.
8. Sprinkle with vegan parmesan cheese (if desired) and serve hot.
9. Enjoy your delicious, plant-based, whole vegan tomato bruschetta made in the air fryer!

6. AIR FRYER VEGAN QUICHE

Servings|4Time|30 minutes

Nutritional Content (per serving):

Cal |295Fat |7.9g Protein |10.3g   Carbs| 11g Fibre| 2.1g

Ingredients:

- 100 grams (1/2 cup) of raw cashews, soaked in water for at least 2 hours or overnight
- 250 ml(1/2 cup) of water
- 1 tbsp (15 ml) of lemon juice
- 2 cloves garlic
- 4 grams (1/2 tsp) of salt
- 2 grams (1/4 tsp) of black pepper
- 4 grams (1/2 tsp) of dried thyme
- 4 grams (1/2 tsp) of dried basil
- 4 grams (1/2 tsp) of turmeric
- 100 grams (1/2 cup) of nutritional yeast
- 125 ml (1/2 cup) of almond milk
- 1 refrigerated pie crust
- 200 grams (1 cup) of sliced mushrooms
- 100 grams (1/2 cup) of chopped red bell pepper
- 100 grams (1/2 cup) of chopped onion
- 15 ml (1 tbsp) of olive oil
- 1 grain (1 pinch) of salt
- 1 grain (1 pinch) of black pepper to taste

Directions:

1. Start by preheating your air fryer to a temperature of 190°C (375°F).
2. In a blender, blend together the soaked cashews, water, lemon juice, garlic, salt, black pepper, thyme, basil, turmeric, nutritional yeast, and plant-based milk until smooth.
3. Roll out the pie crust and fit it into a 9-inch (23 cm) pie dish.
4. In a pan, heat the olive oil over medium heat. Add the mushrooms, red bell pepper, and onion and sauté until you get a tender mixture, about 5 minutes.
5. Pour the cashew mixture over the vegetables in the pan and stir to combine.
6. Pour the mixture into the pie crust in the pie dish.
7. Place the pie dish in the air fryer basket and cook for 25-30 minutes or until the quiche is golden brown and set.
8. Remove the quiche from the air fryer and let it cool for 5 minutes before slicing and serving. Enjoy!

> **Note**: You can use any vegetables you like in this recipe, such as spinach, kale, or zucchini. Feel free to add any spices or herbs you like as well.

7. VEGAN FRITTATA

Servings 3-4 Time | 25 minutes

Nutritional Content (per serving):

Cal |267 Fat |7g Protein |10.3g   Carbs| 15g Fibre| 2 g

Ingredients:

- ❖ 1 block (400 grams/14 ounces) of extra firm tofu
- ❖ 60 ml (1/4 cup) plant-based milk
- ❖ 60 ml (1/4 cup) nutritional yeast
- ❖ 1 tablespoon (8 grams) cornstarch
- ❖ 1 teaspoon turmeric
- ❖ 1 teaspoon garlic powder
- ❖ 1 teaspoon onion powder
- ❖ 1 pinch of salt
- ❖ Ground black pepper, to taste
- ❖ 15 ml (1 tablespoon) olive oil
- ❖ 1 red bell pepper, diced
- ❖ 1 yellow onion, diced
- ❖ 200 grams (7 ounces/1 cup) sliced mushrooms
- ❖ 500 grams (17.5 ounces/2 1/2 cups) chopped kale or spinach
- ❖ 4 grams (1/2 teaspoon) dried basil.

Directions:

1. Start by preheating your air fryer to a temperature of 190°C (375°F).
2. In a bowl, crumble the tofu with your hands.
3. Add the plant-based milk, nutritional yeast, cornstarch, turmeric, garlic powder, onion powder, salt, and pepper to the bowl with the tofu and mix well.
4. In a medium pan, heat the olive oil over a medium heat; then add in the red bell pepper, the yellow onion, and the mushrooms and sauté until everything becomes tender, for about 5 minutes.
5. Add the kale or spinach and dried basil to the pan and stir until the greens are wilted.
6. Pour the tofu mixture into the pan with the vegetables and stir to combine.
7. Pour the mixture into a 9-inch (23 cm) pie dish.
8. Place the dish in the air fryer basket and cook for 20-25 minutes, or until the frittata is golden brown and set.
9. Remove the frittata from the air fryer and let it cool for 5 minutes before slicing and serving. Enjoy!

> ➢ **Note:** You can use any vegetables you like in this recipe, such as diced zucchini, cherry tomatoes, or roasted red pepper. Feel free to add any spices or herbs you like as well.

8. VEGAN AIR FRIED MAC AND CHEESE

Servings|4 Time|15 minutes

Nutritional Content (per serving):

Cal |297Fat |7.5g Protein |11.3g   Carbs| 16g Fibre| 1.8g

Ingredients:

- 30 grams (8 ounces) of whole grain macaroni
- 250 ml (1 cup) of unsweetened almond milk
- 50 grams (1/4 cup) nutritional yeast
- 30 grams (1/8 cup, 2 tablespoons) of all-purpose flour
- 15 ml (1 tablespoon) of olive oil
- 2 teaspoons Dijon mustard

- 8 grams (1 teaspoon) garlic powder
- 8 grams (1 teaspoon) of onion powder
- 4 grams (1/2 teaspoon) of turmeric
- 1 grain (1 pinch) of salt and pepper to taste
- 50 grams (1/4 cup) of breadcrumbs

Directions:

1. Cook your macaroni according to the instructions of the package.
2. In a medium heavy saucepan, heat your olive oil over a medium heat.
3. Whisk in the flour and cook for 1 minute, or until the mixture becomes a paste.
4. Gradually add the almond milk, whisking constantly, and cook for 2-3 minutes, or until the mixture thickens.
5. Remove from heat and stir in the nutritional yeast, Dijon mustard, garlic powder, onion powder, turmeric, salt, and pepper.
6. Add in your cooked macaroni to your already prepared sauce and stir very well to combine.
7. Transfer the mixture to an oven-safe dish and sprinkle with breadcrumbs.
8. Place the dish in the air fryer and cook at 200° C (400°F) for 10-15 minutes, or until the breadcrumbs are golden brown and the mac and cheese is heated through.
9. Serve hot and enjoy!

9. AIR FRYER VEGAN TOFU SANDWICHES

Servings|4 Time|10 minutes

Nutritional Content (per serving):

Cal |256Fat |10g Protein |12g Carbs| 13g Fibre| 1.9 g

Ingredients:

- ❖ 2 slices of whole grain bread
- ❖ 1/2 block of firm tofu
- ❖ 15 ml (1 tablespoon) olive oil
- ❖ 1 grain (1 pinch) of salt

- ❖ 1 tomato, sliced
- ❖ 1 avocado, sliced
- ❖ 1 handful of lettuce leaves
- ❖ 1 grain (1 pinch) of ground black pepper to taste

Directions:

1. Start by draining the tofu and slice it into thick pieces.
2. In a shallow dish, mix the olive oil, salt, and pepper.
3. Coat each piece of tofu in the olive oil mixture.
4. Place the coated tofu slices in the air fryer basket in a single layer.
5. Cook at 200°C (400°F) for about 8-10 minutes, flipping the tofu halfway through, or until it is crispy and golden brown.
6. Toast the bread in the air fryer. Assemble the sandwich by layering the tofu, tomato, avocado, and lettuce between the two slices of bread.
7. Serve hot and enjoy!

> **Note:** You may need to adjust the cooking time based on the size and model of your air fryer. You can also add additional seasonings or condiments of your choice to the sandwich to suit your taste preferences.

10. VEGAN BREAKFAST POTATO HASH

Servings|2-3 Time|20 minutes

Nutritional Content (per serving):

Cal |270 Fat |10g Protein |8g Carbs| 11.5g Fibre| 1.3g

Ingredients:

- ❖ 2 medium sweet potatoes, peeled and diced
- ❖ 1 red onion, diced
- ❖ 1 red bell pepper, diced
- ❖ 1 yellow bell pepper, diced
- ❖ 15ml (1 tablespoon) of olive oil
- ❖ 8 grams (1 teaspoon) of paprika
- ❖ 1 teaspoon of garlic powder
- ❖ 8 grams (1 teaspoon) of onion powder
- ❖ 1 grain (1 pinch) of salt
- ❖ 1 grain (1 pinch) of ground black pepper

Directions:

1. In a large bowl, mix the diced sweet potatoes, red onion, red bell pepper, yellow bell pepper, olive oil, paprika, garlic powder, onion powder, salt, and pepper.
2. Transfer the mixture to the air fryer basket in a single layer.
3. Cook at 200°C (400°F) for 15-20 minutes, stirring halfway through, or until the sweet potatoes are tender and the vegetables are slightly charred.
4. Serve hot as a side dish or topped with additional toppings of your choice, such as avocado, salsa, or hot sauce.

> **Note:** You may need to adjust the cooking time based on the size and model of your air fryer.

11.   VEGAN CINNAMON OATMEAL

Servings|2 Time|20 minutes

Nutritional Content (per serving):

Cal |130Fat |4g Protein |3g   Carbs| 15g Fibre| 1.3g

Ingredients:

- 200 grams (1 cup) of old-fashioned oats
- 500 ml (2 cups) of water
- 8 grams (1 teaspoon) of cinnamon
- 8 ml (½ tablespoon) of unsweetened vanilla extract
- A grain (1 pinch) of salt
- 200 grams (1 cup) of fresh fruit and nuts for topping (optional)

Directions:

1. In a medium saucepan, combine the oats, water, cinnamon, vanilla extract, and salt. Stir very well to combine.
2. Cook the mixture over medium heat, stirring occasionally, until it comes to a simmer.
3. Remove the saucepan from heat and let the oatmeal cool for a few minutes.
4. Spoon the oatmeal mixture into a heat-resistant dish that will fit in your air fryer.
5. Place the dish in the air fryer and set the temperature to 170° C (330°F).
6. Cook the oatmeal for 20 minutes, stirring every 5 minutes.
7. Remove the dish from the air fryer and let it cool for a few minutes.
8. Serve the oatmeal with fresh fruit and nuts, if desired. Enjoy!

12.   VEGAN POLENTA

Servings|3 Time|15 minutes

Nutritional Content (per serving):

Cal |130Fat |6g Protein |6g   Carbs| 12g Fibre| 1.3g

Ingredients:

- ❖ 200 grams (1 cup) cornmeal
- ❖ 1 liter (4 cups) of water
- ❖ 2 grams (1/4 teaspoon) of salt
- ❖ 30 ml (2 tablespoons) of olive oil
- ❖ Optional: add-ins like herbs, spices, or vegan cheese

Directions:

1. In a medium heavy saucepan, bring the water and the salt to a boil.
2. Gradually add in your cornmeal, whisking constantly to prevent lumps.
3. Reduce the heat to low and continue to cook, stirring frequently, until the mixture is thick, about 10 minutes.
4. Stir in the olive oil and any desired add-ins.
5. Pour your mixture into a greased air fryer basket and smooth it out evenly.
6. Air fry at 200°C (400°F) for 15 minutes, or until the top is golden and crispy.
7. Serve hot with your favorite toppings, like marinara sauce, sautéed vegetables, or vegan sour cream.
8. Enjoy your sugar-free vegan air fryer polenta!

13. SUGAR FREE AIR FRYER COCOA PUDDING

Servings|2 Time|10minutes

Nutritional Content (per serving):

Cal |138Fat |3g Protein |8g   Carbs| 14g Fibre| 1.5g

Ingredients:

- ❖ 1 avocado, peeled and pitted
- ❖ 100 grams (1/2 cup) of unsweetened cocoa powder
- ❖ 60 ml (¼ cup) of almond milk
- ❖ 30 ml (2 tablespoons) of maple syrup or your preferred sugar-free sweetener
- ❖ 8 grams (1 teaspoon) of unsweetened vanilla extract
- ❖ Optional: toppings such as fresh berries, coconut flakes, or vegan whipped cream

Directions:

1. In a blender or in a food processor, combine all together the avocado, with the cocoa powder, almond milk, maple syrup or sweetener, and vanilla extract. Blend until smooth.
2. Pour the mixture into a greased air fryer basket.
3. Air fry at a temperature of 200°C (400°F) for 10 minutes, or until the pudding is set.
4. Serve the pudding warm with your desired toppings.
5. Enjoy your breakfast!

14.   VEGAN AIR FRYER GRANOLA

Servings|4 Time|15 minutes

Nutritional Content (per serving):

Cal |225Fat |6.5g Protein |8.3g   Carbs| 13g Fibre| 1.6g

Ingredients:

- ❖ 500 grams (2 ½ cups) of rolled oats
- ❖ 200 grams (1 cup) of chopped almonds, pecans, or walnuts, etc.
- ❖ 100 grams (1/2 cup) of unsweetened coconut flakes

- ❖ 30 ml (2 tablespoons) of melted coconut oil
- ❖ 30 ml (2 tablespoons) of sugar-free sweetener (such as stevia or erythritol)
- ❖ 8 ml (1/2 tablespoon) of vanilla extract
- ❖ 1 grain (1 pinch) of teaspoon salt
- ❖ Optional: dried fruits, such as cranberries or raisins, for serving

Directions:

1. In a large deep bowl, combine all the oats with the nuts, and the coconut flakes.
2. In a small bowl, whisk all together the coconut oil, with the sugar-free sweetener, the vanilla extract, and the salt.
3. Pour the oil mixture over the oats mixture and stir until well combined.
4. Spread the mixture evenly in the basket of your air fryer.
5. Air fry at a temperature of about 200°C (400°F) for 10-15 minutes, or until the granola is golden and crispy, stirring every 5 minutes.
6. Let the granola cool completely in the air fryer basket.
7. Serve the granola with dried fruit, if desired.
8. This sugar-free vegan air fryer granola is a healthy and delicious snack that's easy to make. Enjoy!

15. SUGAR FREE QUINOA BREAKFAST

Servings|3-4Time|15 minutes

Nutritional Content (per serving):

Cal |220Fat |10g Protein |9g   Carbs| 16g Fibre| 2 g

Ingredients:

- ❖ 200 grams (1 cup) of quinoa
- ❖ 500 ml (2 cups) of water
- ❖ 1 grain (1 pinch) of salt
- ❖ 200 grams (1 cup) of fresh strawberries, finely diced
- ❖ 30 ml (2 tablespoons) of sugar-free sweetener (such as stevia or erythritol)
- ❖ 8 ml (1/2 tablespoon) of lemon juice
- ❖ 8 ml (1/2 tablespoon) of vanilla extract
- ❖ Optional: fresh mint leaves for garnish

Directions:

1. Start by rinsing the quinoa in a fine-mesh strainer and place it in a saucepan with the water and salt.
2. Bring the mixture to a boil, and then reduce the heat to low and cover. Cook until the quinoa is tender, and the water is absorbed, about 15-20 minutes.
3. While the quinoa is cooking, in a separate bowl, mix the strawberries, sugar-free sweetener, lemon juice, and vanilla extract.
4. Once the quinoa is cooked, transfer it to a bowl and stir in the strawberry mixture.
5. Place the quinoa mixture in the air fryer basket and air fry at 200°c (400°F) for 10-15 minutes, or until the quinoa is heated through and the strawberries are slightly softened.
6. Serve the quinoa warm, garnished with fresh mint leaves, if desired.

> **Note:**

This sugar-free strawberry air fryer quinoa is a healthy and delicious dish that's easy to make. Enjoy!

16. POTATOES AND COCONUT CREAM BOWL

Servings|4 Time|25 minutes

Nutritional Content (per serving):

Cal |125Fat |8g Protein |8g Carbs| 13g Fibre| 1.6g

Ingredients:

- 4 medium potatoes, sliced
- 30 ml (2 tablespoons) of melted coconut oil
- 1 grain (1 pinch) of salt
- 1 grain (1 pinch) of ground black pepper, to taste
- 100 grams (1/2 cup) of coconut cream
- 15 ml (1 tablespoon) of sugar-free sweetener (such as stevia or erythritol)
- 8 ml (1/2 tablespoon) of lemon juice
- 8 grams (1 teaspoon) of dried thyme

Directions:

1. In a large bowl, toss the sliced potatoes with the melted coconut oil, salt, and pepper.
2. Arrange your potatoes in one single layer in your air fryer basket.
3. Air fry at a temperature of about 200° C (400°F) for about 20 to 25 minutes, or until the potatoes are tender and crispy, flipping once halfway through.
4. In a separate bowl, whisk together the coconut cream, sugar-free sweetener, lemon juice, and dried thyme.
5. Serve the potatoes with the coconut cream sauce drizzled over the top.
6. Serve and enjoy your breakfast!

17. BREAKFAST BURRITOS

Servings|4 Time|7 minutes

Nutritional Content (per serving):

Cal |250Fat |12g Protein |9.3g Carbs| 10.2g Fibre| 1.5g

Ingredients:

- 4 large flour tortillas
- 200 grams (1 cup) of cooked black beans
- 200 grams (1 cup) of cooked brown rice
- 1 avocado, diced
- 200 grams (1 cup) of diced tomatoes
- 200 grams (1 cup) of shredded lettuce

- 100 grams (1/2 cup) diced red onion
- 30 grams (2 tablespoons) of diced jalapeno pepper
- 30 ml (2 tablespoons) of lime juice
- 8 grams (1 teaspoon) of chili powder
- 1 grain (1 pinch) of salt
- 1 grain (1 pinch) of ground black pepper, to taste
- 250 ml (1 cup) of sugar-free salsa, for serving

Directions:

1. Lay each tortilla flat and spread a quarter of the black beans, rice, avocado, tomatoes, lettuce, red onion, and jalapeno pepper in a line down the center.
2. Sprinkle the lime juice, chili powder, salt, and pepper over the fillings.
3. Roll up each tortilla tightly, tucking in the ends.
4. Place the burritos in the air fryer basket and air fry at 200°C (400°F) for 5-7 minutes, or until the tortillas are crispy.
5. Serve the burritos with sugar-free salsa on the side.
6. Enjoy your breakfast!

18. LEEK AND MUSHROOM OMELET

Servings|2 Time|4 minutes

Nutritional Content (per serving):

Cal |171Fat |8g Protein |15 g Carbs| 15g Fibre| 1.3g

Ingredients:

- 200 grams (1 cup) of rolled oats
- 450 grams (1 pound) of unsweetened almond milk
- 15 ml (1 tablespoon) of sugar-free sweetener (such as stevia or erythritol)

- 8 ml (1/2 tablespoon) of vanilla extract
- 1 grain (1 pinch) of salt
- Optional toppings: diced fruit, chopped nuts, shredded coconut

Directions:

1. In a large bowl, mix together the oats, almond milk, sugar-free sweetener, vanilla extract, and salt.
2. Place the mixture in a heat-safe dish that fits in the air fryer basket.
3. Air fry at a temperature of about 170° C (330°F) for 15-20 minutes, stirring occasionally, or until the porridge is thick and creamy.
4. Serve the porridge warm, topped with diced fruit, chopped nuts, shredded coconut, or any other toppings of your choice.
5. This sugar-free vegan air fryer porridge is a healthy and delicious breakfast that's easy to make.
6. Enjoy your breakfast!

19.   CHICKPEAS AND SHALLOTS BOWL

Servings|4 Time|30 minutes

Nutritional Content (per serving):

Cal |125Fat |6.3 g Protein |8g   Carbs| 13g Fibre| 1.4g

Ingredients:

- ❖ 250 gram (1/2 pound, 1 can) of chickpeas, drained and rinsed
- ❖ 30 ml (2 tablespoons) of olive oil
- ❖ 1 grain (1 pinch) of salt
- ❖ 1 grain (1 pinch of ground black pepper) to taste

- ❖ 2 large shallots, thinly sliced
- ❖ 15 ml (1 tablespoon) of lemon juice
- ❖ 8 grams (1 teaspoon) of dried thyme

Directions:

1. In a large deep bowl, toss all together the chickpeas with the olive oil, the salt, and the ground black pepper.
2. Arrange your seasoned chickpeas in one single layer in your air fryer basket.
3. Air fry at a temperature of about 200° C (400°F) for about 20 to 25 minutes, or until the chickpeas become crispy; make sure to flip once halfway through.
4. In a separate bowl, mix all together the shallots, with the lemon juice, the thyme, the salt, and the pepper.
5. Add the shallot mixture to the air fryer basket for the last 5 minutes of cooking.
6. Serve the chickpeas and the shallots warm.
7. Serve and enjoy your breakfast!

20.   PUMPKIN OATMEAL

Servings|4 Time|20 minutes

Nutritional Content (per serving):

Cal |245Fat |12.6g Protein |8g   Carbs| 12g Fibre| 1.7g

Ingredients:

- ❖ 200 grams (1 cup) of rolled oats
- ❖ 350 ml (1 1/2 cups) of unsweetened almond milk
- ❖ 100 grams (1/2 cup) of pure pumpkin puree
- ❖ 15 ml (1 tablespoon) of sugar-free sweetener (such as stevia or erythritol)

- ❖ 8 grams (1 teaspoon) of pumpkin pie spice
- ❖ 1 grain (1 pinch) of salt
- ❖ Optional toppings: diced fruit, chopped nuts, shredded coconut

Directions:

1. In a large deep bowl, mix all together the oats, with the almond milk, the pumpkin puree, sugar-free sweetener, the pumpkin pie spice, and the salt.
2. Place your mixture in a heat-safe dish that fits in your air fryer basket.
3. Air fry at a temperature of about 170° C (330°F) for about 15 to 20 minutes, stirring occasionally, or until the oatmeal is thick and creamy.
4. Serve the oatmeal warm, topped with diced fruit, chopped nuts, shredded coconut, or any other toppings of your choice.
5. This sugar-free vegan air fryer pumpkin oatmeal is a healthy and delicious breakfast that's easy to make. Enjoy!

VEGAN PLANT BASED AIR FRYER APPETIZERS

21.   VEGAN AIR FRYER HUSH PUPPIES

Servings|4 Time|12 minutes

Nutritional Content (per serving):

Cal |235Fat |10.3g Protein |9.3 g   Carbs| 13g Fibre| 1.5g

Ingredients:

- 200 grams (1 cup) of yellow cornmeal
- 100 grams (1/2 cup) of all-purpose flour
- 15 grams (1 tablespoon) of baking powder
- 1 grain (1 pinch) of salt
- 1 grain (1 pinch) of black pepper
- 15 ml (1 tablespoon) of cooking spray

- 125 ml (1/2 cup) of unsweetened almond milk
- 30 grams (1/4 cup) of finely chopped onion
- 30 grams (1/4 cup) of finely chopped green pepper
- 15 grams (1 tablespoon) of chopped fresh parsley
- 15 grams (1 tablespoon) of ground flaxseed mixed with 45 ml (3 tablespoons) of water

Directions:

1. In a large and deep mixing bowl, whisk all together the cornmeal, with the flour, baking powder, salt, and black pepper.
2. Add the almond milk, the onion, the green pepper, the parsley; and the flaxseed mixture. Stir until everything is very well combined.
3. Preheat your air fryer to a temperature of about 190°C (375°F).
4. With the help of a small cookie scoop or spoon, drop the batter into your air fryer basket.
5. Lightly spray your hush puppies with cooking spray.
6. Air fry for about 10 to 12 minutes or until your hush puppies get a golden brown and become crispy.
7. Serve hot with your favorite dipping sauce.
8. Enjoy your delicious and healthier vegan hush puppies!

22.   AIR FRYER BEETS

Servings|2 Time|15 minutes

Nutritional Content (per serving):

Cal |103Fat |3 g Protein |4.3g   Carbs| 8 g Fibre| 1g

Ingredients:

- ❖ 4 medium-sized beets, peeled and cut into wedges
- ❖ 15 ml (1 tablespoon) of olive oil

- ❖ 1 grain (1 pinch) of salt
- ❖ 1 grain (1 pinch) of ground black pepper
- ❖ 4 grams (1/2 teaspoon) of dried thyme

Directions:

1. Start by preheating your air fryer to a temperature of about 190°C (375°F).
2. In a large mixing bowl, toss the beet wedges with olive oil, salt, black pepper, and thyme until the beets are well coated.
3. Place the beets in the air fryer basket, making sure they are not touching each other.
4. Air fry for about 10 to 15 minutes, shaking the basket every 5 minutes, until the beets are perfectly tender and crispy on the outside.
5. Serve your appetizer hot as a side dish or add them to your favorite salad.
6. Enjoy your delicious, sugar-free, and easy-to-make air fryer vegan beets!

23.   AIR FRYER POTATO WEDGES

Servings|2 Time|20 minutes

Nutritional Content (per serving):

Cal |325Fat |8 g Protein |8g Carbs| 12g Fibre| 1.3 g

Ingredients:

- ❖ 2 to 3 large potatoes, scrubbed and cut into wedges
- ❖ 30 ml (2 tablespoons) of olive oil
- ❖ 8 grams (1 teaspoon) of garlic powder
- ❖ 8 grams (1 teaspoon) of onion powder
- ❖ 8 grams (1 teaspoon) of paprika
- ❖ 4 grams (1/2 teaspoon) of salt
- ❖ 2 grams (1/4 teaspoon) of ground black pepper

Directions:

1. Preheat your air fryer to a temperature of 200°C (400°F).
2. In a large mixing bowl, toss all together the potato wedges with the olive oil, the garlic powder, the onion powder, the paprika, the salt, and the ground black pepper until the potatoes are well coated.
3. Place the potato wedges in your air fryer basket, making sure they are not touching each other.
4. Air fry for 15 to about 20 minutes; make sure to shake the basket every 5 minutes, or until the potatoes become crispy and golden brown on the outside and tender on the inside.
5. Serve your potato wedges hot with your favorite dipping sauce.
6. Enjoy your delicious and easy-to-make air fryer vegan potato wedges!

24. AVOCADO ROLLS

Servings|4 Time|10 minutes

Nutritional Content (per serving):

Cal |285Fat |9g Protein |8g Carbs| 12g Fibre| 1.7 g

Ingredients:

- 2 large ripe avocados, pitted and sliced
- 8-10 rice paper wrappers
- 100 grams (1/2 cup) of shredded carrots
- 100 grams (1/2 cup) of sliced cucumber
- 100 grams (1/2 cup) of sliced bell peppers
- 50 grams (1/4 cup) of chopped fresh cilantro
- 50 grams (1/4 cup) of chopped scallions
- 1 grain (1 pinch) of salt
- 1 grain (1 pinch) of ground black pepper, to taste
- Cooking spray

Directions:

1. Preheat your air fryer to a temperature of about 200°C (400°F).
2. In a large mixing bowl, combine all together the sliced avocados, the shredded carrots, the sliced cucumber, the sliced bell peppers, the cilantro, scallions, the salt, and the ground black pepper. Mix your ingredients very well.
3. Fill a large shallow dish with warm water. Dip one rice paper wrapper into the water for a few seconds, until it is pliable.
4. Place the wet rice paper wrapper on a clean work surface. Spoon 2-3 tablespoons of the avocado mixture onto the center of the wrapper.
5. Fold the bottom of the wrapper up over the filling, then fold the sides in and roll up tightly to seal.
6. Repeat the same process with the remaining rice paper wrappers and with the filling.
7. Lightly spray the avocado rolls with cooking spray; then place them in your air fryer basket in one single layer.
8. Air fry for about 8-10 minutes or until your rolls become golden brown and crispy.
9. Serve your rolls hot with your favorite dipping sauce.
10. Enjoy your delicious and healthier vegan air fryer avocado rolls!

25. WHOLE VEGAN AIR FRYER SAMOSA

Servings|4 Time|10 minutes

Nutritional Content (per serving):

Cal |250Fat |10.6g Protein |8.7g Carbs| 13.5g Fibre| 1.7 g

Ingredients:

- ❖ 100 grams (1/2 cup) of vegan cheese, grated
- ❖ 50 grams (1/4 cup) of finely chopped onion
- ❖ 50 grams (1/4 cup) of finely chopped bell peppers
- ❖ 4 grams (1/2 teaspoon) of cumin powder
- ❖ 4 grams (1/2 teaspoon) of coriander powder
- ❖ 4 grams (1/2 teaspoon) of salt
- ❖ 2 grams (1/4 teaspoon) of ground black pepper
- ❖ 10 samosa wrappers
- ❖ 15 ml (1 tablespoon) of cooking spray

Directions:

1. In a large deep mixing bowl, combine the grated vegan cheese, chopped onion, chopped bell peppers, cumin powder, coriander powder, salt, and black pepper. Mix very well.
2. Lay a samosa wrapper on a clean work surface with one corner pointing towards you. Brush the edges of your wrappers with the water.
3. Place a tablespoon of the cheese filling on the bottom corner of the wrapper.
4. Fold the bottom corner over the filling; then fold the wrapper diagonally to create a triangle. Continue folding the triangle up, maintaining the triangle shape, until you reach the end of the wrapper. Press the edges to seal.
5. Repeat with the remaining samosa wrappers and filling.
6. Preheat your air fryer to a temperature of about 190°C (375°F).
7. Lightly spray the samosas with cooking spray and place them in the air fryer basket in a single layer.
8. Air fry for about 8 to 10 minutes, flipping the samosas halfway through, until golden brown and crispy.
9. Serve hot with your favorite dipping sauce.
10. Enjoy your delicious and easy-to-make vegan cheese samosas!

26.   KALE AND POTATO NUGGETS

Servings| 4Time|12 minutes
Nutritional Content (per serving):
Cal |165 Fat | 8g Protein |8.6g   Carbs| 10g Fibre| 1.3g

Ingredients:

- 400 grams (2 cups, 1 pound) of kale, finely chopped
- 2 cups of potatoes, peeled and grated
- 100 grams (1/2 cup) of breadcrumbs
- 50 grams (1/4 cup) of flour
- 50 grams (1/4 cup) of nutritional yeast

- 8 grams (1 teaspoon) of garlic powder
- 8 grams (1 teaspoon) of onion powder
- 4 grams (1/2 teaspoon) of salt
- 2 grams (1/4 teaspoon) of ground black pepper
- 15 ml (1 tablespoon) of cooking spray

Directions:

1. In a large mixing bowl, combine the chopped kale, grated potatoes, breadcrumbs, flour, nutritional yeast, garlic powder, onion powder, salt, and black pepper. Mix well.
2. Using your hands, form the mixture into small nugget-shaped balls.
3. Preheat your air fryer to a temperature of 200°C (400°F).
4. Lightly spray the nuggets with cooking spray and place them in the air fryer basket in a single layer.
5. Air fry for about 10-12 minutes, flipping the nuggets halfway through, until golden brown and crispy.
6. Serve your appetizer hot with your favorite dipping sauce.
7. Enjoy your delicious and nutritious vegan kale and potato nuggets!

27. VEGAN CHICKPEA MEATBALLS

Servings| 5Time|15minutes

Nutritional Content (per serving):

Cal | 198Fat | 13g Protein |9g   Carbs| 11g Fibre| 1.6g

Ingredients:

- ❖ 1 can (15 oz, 1 pound) of chickpeas, drained and rinsed
- ❖ 100 grams (1/2 cup) of panko breadcrumbs
- ❖ 50 grams(1/4 cup) of chopped onion
- ❖ 2 cloves garlic, minced

- ❖ 1 5 grams (2 tablespoons) of nutritional yeast
- ❖ 15 ml (1 tablespoon) of soy sauce
- ❖ 15 ml (1 tablespoon) of tomato paste
- ❖ 8 grams (1 teaspoon) dried oregano
  Salt and black pepper, to taste

Directions:

1. Preheat your air fryer to a temperature of 190°C (375°F).
2. In a food processor, pulse the chickpeas until they are crumbly.
3. Add the panko breadcrumbs, chopped onion, minced garlic, nutritional yeast, soy sauce, tomato paste, dried oregano, salt, and black pepper. Pulse until combined.
4. Use your hands to form the mixture into 12 equal-sized meatballs.
5. Spray the meatballs with cooking spray and place them in the air fryer basket.
6. Air fry for 12-15 minutes, or until the meatballs are golden brown and crispy on the outside.
7. Serve the meatballs as desired, such as with marinara sauce, on top of pasta, or in a sandwich. Enjoy!

28. AIR FRYER ACORN SQUASH

Servings| 4Time|15minutes
Nutritional Content (per serving):
Cal | 158 Fat | 3.8g Protein |3.5g Carbs| 15g Fibre| 1.4g

Ingredients:

- ❖ 1 acorn squash
- ❖ 1 tablespoon olive oil
- ❖ 1/2 teaspoon salt

- ❖ 2 grams (1/4 teaspoon) of ground black pepper
- ❖ 4 grams (1/2 teaspoon) of paprika

Directions:

1. Preheat your air fryer to a temperature of 200°C (400°F).
2. Cut the acorn squash in half, remove the seeds, and slice each half into 1/2-inch wedges.
3. In a small bowl, whisk together olive oil, salt, black pepper, and paprika.
4. Place the acorn squash wedges in a large bowl and drizzle the olive oil mixture over them. Toss until the wedges are well coated.
5. Place the wedges in the air fryer basket, making sure they are in a single layer and not touching each other.
6. Air fry for about 12 to 15 minutes, flipping the wedges halfway through cooking time, or until they are tender and lightly browned.
7. Serve your appetizer immediately and enjoy!

29. AIR FRYER VEGAN CALAMARI

Servings| 4 Time|10 minutes
Nutritional Content (per serving):
Cal | 205Fat | 7.5g Protein |4.3g   Carbs| 12g Fibre| 1.8g

Ingredients:

- 450 grams (1 pound) of oyster mushrooms
- 200 grams (1 cup) of all-purpose flour
- 100 grams (1/2 cup) of cornstarch
- 8 grams (1teaspoon) of garlic powder
- 8 grams (1 teaspoon) of paprika

- 1 grain (1 pinch) of salt
- 2 grams (1/4 teaspoon) of ground black pepper
- 250 ml (1 cup) of unsweetened almond milk
- 15 ml (1 tablespoon) of apple cider vinegar
- 15 ml (1 tablespoon) of Cooking spray

Directions:

1. Preheat your air fryer to a temperature of 190° C (375°F).
2. Cut the oyster mushrooms into thin strips, resembling the shape of calamari rings.
3. In a large bowl, whisk all together the flour, with the cornstarch, the garlic powder, the paprika, salt, and black pepper.
4. In a separate bowl, mix the plant-based milk and apple cider vinegar.
5. Dip the mushroom strips into the milk mixture; then coat them with the flour mixture, shaking off any excess.
6. Lightly coat your air fryer basket with cooking spray, then place the mushroom strips in a single layer.
7. Air fry for about 8 to 10 minutes, or until the strips are golden brown and crispy.
8. Serve your appetizer immediately and enjoy with your favorite dipping sauce!

30. POTATO PATTIES

Servings| 3 Time|7 minutes
Nutritional Content (per serving):
Cal | 230 Fat | 10.3g Protein |6g   Carbs| 12g Fibre| 1.4 g

Ingredients:

- 2 large potatoes, peeled and boiled until soft
- 100 grams (1/2 cup) of breadcrumbs
- 50 grams (1/4 cup) of finely chopped onion
- 50 grams (1/4 cup) of chopped fresh parsley

- 1 grain (1pinch) of salt
- 1 grain (1 pinch) of black pepper
- 1 grain (1 pinch) of paprika
- 2 grams (1/4 teaspoon) of garlic powder
- 15 ml (1 tablespoon) of Cooking spray

Directions:

1. Preheat your air fryer to a temperature of about 200°C (400°F).
2. In a large deep bowl, mash the boiled potatoes.
3. Add the breadcrumbs, the onion, parsley, salt, pepper, paprika, and garlic powder to the bowl, and mix until your ingredients are very well combined.
4. Shape your mixture into about 8 to 10 patties, about 2 inches in diameter each.
5. Spray your air fryer basket with cooking spray; then arrange your patties in your Air Fryer basket, making sure they don't touch.
6. Air fries your patties for about 10 to 12 minutes, making sure to flip them halfway through, until they are golden brown and crispy on both sides.
7. Serve hot and enjoy your patties hot!

31.   AIR FRYER PLANTAINS

Servings| 2 Time|10 minutes

Nutritional Content (per serving):

Cal | 225 Fat | 4g Protein |2g Carbs| 18g Fibre| 1.8g

Ingredients:

- ❖ 2 ripe plantains, peeled and sliced into 1/2-inch pieces
- ❖ 15 ml (1 tablespoon) of olive oil or cooking spray
- ❖ 1 grain (1 pinch) of salt

Directions:

1. Preheat your air fryer to a temperature of about 190° C (375°F).
2. Toss the plantain slices in olive oil or spray them with cooking spray.
3. Sprinkle the salt and any other seasonings you prefer over the plantains.
4. Place the plantain slices in a single layer in the air fryer basket.
5. Air fry for about 8 to 10 minutes, making sure to flip the plantains over halfway through, until they are crispy and golden brown.
6. Remove the plantains from the air fryer and let them cool for a few minutes before serving.
7. Enjoy your appetizer!

32.   LENTIL MEATBALLS

Servings| 4 Time|30 minutes
Nutritional Content (per serving):
Cal | 130 Fat | 12g Protein |7g   Carbs| 10.6g Fibre| 1.8g

Ingredients:

- 200 grams (1 cup) of dry lentils
- 450 grams (2 ½ cups) of vegetable broth
- 100 grams (1/2 cup) of rolled oats
- 50 grams (1/4 cup) of chopped onion
- 2 cloves garlic, minced
- 15 grams (1 tablespoon) of ground flaxseed

- 45 ml (3 tablespoons) of water
- 15 grams (2 tablespoons) of nutritional yeast
- 8 grams (1 teaspoon) of dried basil
- 8 grams (1 teaspoon) of dried of oregano
- 1 grain (1/2 teaspoon) of salt
- 2 grams (¼ teaspoon) of ground black pepper
- 15 ml (1 heap tablespoon) of vegetable, like extra virgin olive oil

Directions:

1. Preheat your air fryer to a temperature of 190° C (375°F).
2. Rinse and drain the lentils. In a medium deep saucepan and bring the vegetable broth to a boil. Add the lentils to your saucepan and reduce the heat to a simmer; then let cook the lentils for about 25 to 30 minutes, or until they're tender and the liquid is absorbed.
3. In a large bowl, mix the rolled oats, chopped onion, minced garlic, flaxseed, water, nutritional yeast, dried basil, dried oregano, salt, and black pepper.
4. Once the lentils are done cooking, add them to the bowl and mix everything together. Mash the lentils a little bit to help everything stick together.
5. Form the lentil mixture into golf-ball sized meatballs.
6. Brush the meatballs with olive oil.
7. Place the meatballs in the air fryer basket in a single layer, and air fry them for 10-12 minutes, or until they're golden brown and crispy on the outside.
8. Serve the lentil meatballs with your favorite sauce or on top of pasta.
9. Enjoy your delicious vegan lentil meatballs made in the air fryer!

33. SPICY BANANA CHIPS

Servings| 2Time|10 minutes
Nutritional Content (per serving):
Cal | 260Fat | 7g Protein |5.6g Carbs| 11g Fibre| 1.8g

Ingredients:

- ❖ 2 ripe bananas
- ❖ 1 grain (1 pinch) of freshly ground black pepper
- ❖ 1 grain (1 pinch) of sea salt
- ❖ 15 ml (1 tablespoon) of cooking spray

Directions:

1. Preheat your air fryer to a temperature of about 170°C (350°F).
2. Peel the bananas and cut them into thin slices, about 1/8 inch thick.
3. In a small bowl, mix all together the black pepper and the sea salt.
4. Lightly spray your air fryer basket with cooking spray.
5. Place the banana slices in a single layer in the air fryer basket. Sprinkle half of the black pepper and salt mixture over the banana slices.
6. Air fry the banana slices for about 8 to10 minutes, or until they're crispy and lightly golden brown.
7. Remove the banana chips from the air fryer basket and sprinkle the remaining black pepper and salt mixture over them.
8. Serve the banana chips as a snack or use them as a topping for yogurt, oatmeal, or smoothie bowls.
9. Enjoy your tasty and healthy air fryer banana chips with black pepper!

34. CHICKPEA FALAFEL

Servings| 5 Time|10 minutes

Nutritional Content (per serving):

Cal | 170Fat | 11g Protein |8.5g Carbs| 15g Fibre| 1.6g

Ingredients:

- ❖ 1 can of 450 grams (1 pound) of chickpeas, drained and rinsed
- ❖ 100 grams (1/2 cup) of fresh parsley leaves
- ❖ 100 grams (1/2 cup) of fresh cilantro leaves
- ❖ 50 grams (1/4 cup) of chopped onion
- ❖ 3 garlic cloves, minced

- ❖ 8 grams (1 teaspoon) of ground cumin
- ❖ 8 grams (1 teaspoon) of ground coriander
- ❖ 4 grams (1/2 teaspoon) of baking powder
- ❖ 1 grain (1 pinch) of salt
- ❖ 1 grain (1 pinch) of ground black pepper
- ❖ 50 grams (about 1/4 cup) of flour, all-purpose
- ❖ 15 ml (1 tablespoon) of Cooking spray

Directions:

1. In a food processor, combine all together the chickpeas with the parsley, the cilantro, the onion, the garlic, the cumin, the coriander, the baking powder, the salt, and the ground black pepper.
2. Process your ingredients until the mixture becomes smooth.
3. Add the flour to the mixture and pulse until it is very well combined.
4. Shape your falafel mixture into balls of small size to your liking. You should get about 17 balls.
5. Preheat your air fryer to a temperature of 170°C (350°F).
6. Lightly spray your air fryer basket with cooking spray.
7. Place the falafel balls in the air fryer basket, making sure to leave some space between them.
8. Air fry your falafel balls for about 8 to 10 minutes, flipping them halfway through the cooking time, until they're golden brown and crispy on the outside.
9. Remove the falafel balls from your air fryer and serve them in pita bread with your favorite toppings, such as hummus, tzatziki sauce, chopped tomatoes, and cucumbers.
10. Enjoy your delicious and healthy air fryer vegan falafel!

35. CABBAGE FRITTERS

Servings| 4 Time|17minutes

Nutritional Content (per serving):

Cal | 260Fat | 13g Protein |11g Carbs| 17g Fibre|1.7g

Ingredients:

- 450 grams (2 cups) of shredded cabbage
- 100 grams (1/2 cup) of chickpea flour
- 4 grams (1/2 teaspoon) of ground cumin
- 4 grams (1/2 teaspoon) of ground coriander
- 2 grams (1/4 teaspoon) of turmeric powder
- 2 grams (1/4 teaspoon) of cayenne pepper (optional)
- 4 grams (1/2 teaspoon) of salt
- 50 grams (1/4 cup) of chopped cilantro
- 50 grams (1/4 cup) of chopped onion
- 100 ml (1/4 cup) of water
- 15 ml (1 tablespoon) of Cooking spray

Directions:

1. In a large bowl, combine the shredded cabbage, chickpea flour, ground cumin, ground coriander, turmeric powder, cayenne pepper, and salt. Mix all of your ingredients in the bowl very well
2. Add the chopped cilantro, chopped onion, and water to the bowl. Mix
3. Preheat your air fryer to a temperature of 175°C (375°F) for 5 minutes.
4. Lightly spray your air fryer basket with cooking spray.
5. Using your hands or a spoon, form the batter into small patties, about 2-3 inches in diameter.
6. Place the fritters in the air fryer basket, leaving a bit of space between them.
7. Air fry the fritters for 10-12 minutes, flipping them halfway through the cooking time, until they're golden brown and crispy on the outside.
8. Remove the fritters from the air fryer and let them cool for a few minutes before serving.
9. Serve the fritters as a side dish or appetizer with your favorite dipping sauce, such as tahini sauce or spicy tomato chutney.
10. Enjoy your delicious and healthy whole vegan air fryer cabbage fritters!

36.   CAULIFLOWER WINGS

Servings| 4-5 Time|20 minutes

Nutritional Content (per serving):

Cal | 190Fat | 7.9g Protein |7.5g Carbs| 12g Fibre| 1.5g

Ingredients:

- ❖ 1 head cauliflower, cut into bite-sized florets
- ❖ 200 grams (1 cup) of all-purpose flour
- ❖ 8 grams (1 teaspoon) of garlic powder
- ❖ 8 grams (1 teaspoon) of paprika
- ❖ 4 grams (1/2 teaspoon) of salt
- ❖ 4 grams (1/2 teaspoon) of black pepper
- ❖ 200 grams (1 cup) of almond milk
- ❖ 200 grams (1 cup) of bread crumbs
- ❖ 15 ml (1 tablespoon) of cooking spray
- ❖ Your favorite vegan wing sauce (such as buffalo or BBQ sauce)

Directions:

1. In a large bowl, mix the all-purpose flour, garlic powder, paprika, salt, and black pepper.
2. Add the plant-based milk to the bowl and stir until you have a smooth batter.
3. Now, put the breadcrumbs in a large separate bowl.
4. Dip each cauliflower floret into the batter, making sure it's well coated.
5. Roll the cauliflower in the breadcrumbs, pressing down to ensure the crumbs stick.
6. Preheat your air fryer to a temperature of about 175°C (390°F) for about 5 minutes.
7. Lightly spray your air fryer basket with the use of cooking spray.
8. Place the breaded cauliflower in the air fryer basket, leaving a bit of space between them.
9. Air fry the cauliflower for 12-15 minutes, flipping them halfway through the cooking time, until they're golden brown and crispy on the outside.
10. Once the cauliflower is done, toss it in your favorite vegan wing sauce to coat.
11. Serve the cauliflower wings with your favorite dipping sauce, such as vegan ranch or blue cheese dressing.
12. Enjoy your delicious and healthy vegan air fryer cauliflower wings!

37.   ROASTED BRUSSELS SPROUTS

Servings| 3 Time|12minutes
Nutritional Content (per serving):
Cal | 123Fat | 10.3 g Protein |10.5g   Carbs| 11g Fibre| 1.3g

Ingredients:

- 450 grams (1 pound) of Brussels sprouts, trimmed and halved
- 15 ml (1 tablespoon) of extra virgin olive oil
- 4 grams (1/2 teaspoon) of garlic powder
- 4 grams (1/2 teaspoon) of onion powder
- 4 grams (1/2 teaspoon) of salt
- 1 grain (1 pinch) of freshly ground black pepper, to taste

Directions:

1. Preheat your air fryer to a temperature of 200°C (400°F).
2. In a bowl, toss the halved Brussels sprouts with the olive oil, garlic powder, onion powder, salt, and black pepper.
3. Arrange your Brussels sprouts in your air fryer basket in one single layer.
4. Cook the Brussels sprouts for about 10 to 12 minutes, shaking the basket every few minutes, until they are crispy and golden brown.
5. Serve the roasted Brussels sprouts hot, with a sprinkle of additional salt or black pepper, if desired.
6. Enjoy your delicious vegan roasted Brussels sprouts!

38. ZUCCHINI CORN FRITTERS

Servings| 2-3 Time|10 minutes

Nutritional Content (per serving):

Cal | 150Fat | 6g Protein |6.3g Carbs| 7.5g Fibre| 2g

Ingredients:

- ❖ 2 medium zucchinis, grated
- ❖ 200 grams (1 cup) of corn kernels
- ❖ 100 grams (1/2 cup) of all-purpose flour
- ❖ 4 grams (1/2 teaspoon) of baking powder

- ❖ 1 grain (1 pinch) of salt
- ❖ 1 grain (1 pinch) of ground black pepper
- ❖ 2 grams (1/4 teaspoon) of garlic powder
- ❖ 2 grams (1/4 teaspoon) of onion powder
- ❖ 15 ml (1 tablespoon) of cooking spray

Directions:

1. Preheat your air fryer to a temperature of 190°C (375°F).
2. In a large bowl, mix all together the grated zucchini and corn kernels.
3. In a separate bowl, whisk together the flour, baking powder, salt, black pepper, garlic powder, and onion powder.
4. Add the flour mixture to the zucchini and corn and stir until well combined.
5. Coat your air fryer basket with cooking spray.
6. Scoop the zucchini mixture in tablespoonfuls and drop onto the air fryer basket, leaving a little space between each fritter.
7. Spray the top of the fritters with cooking spray.
8. Air fry the fritters for 8-10 minutes, flipping halfway through, until they are golden brown and crispy.
9. Serve the zucchini corn fritters hot, with your favorite dipping sauce.
10. Enjoy your delicious vegan zucchini corn fritters made in an air fryer!

39. SMOKEY CHICKPEAS

Servings| 4 Time|10 minutes

Nutritional Content (per serving):

Cal | 185Fat | 10g Protein |10.1g Carbs| 11g Fibre| 2g

Ingredients:

- ❖ 1 can; 450 grams (1pound) of chickpeas, drained and rinsed
- ❖ 15 ml (1 tablespoon) of olive oil
- ❖ 8 grams (1 teaspoon) of smoked paprika
- ❖ 4 grams (1/2 teaspoon) of garlic powder

- ❖ 2 grams (1/4 teaspoon) of onion powder
- ❖ 2 grams (1/4 teaspoon) of salt
- ❖ 2 grams (1/4 teaspoon) of ground black pepper

Directions:

1. Preheat your air fryer to a temperature of about 175°C (380°F).
2. In a bowl, toss all together the chickpeas with olive oil, smoked paprika, garlic powder, onion powder, salt, and black pepper.
3. Place the chickpeas in your air fryer basket in one single layer.
4. Air fry your chickpeas for about 10 to 12 minutes; making sure to shake the basket every few minutes, until they are crispy and golden brown.
5. Serve the smokey chickpeas hot.
6. Enjoy your delicious vegan smokey chickpeas!

40. KALE CHIPS

Servings| 2-3Time|7 minutes

Nutritional Content (per serving):

Cal | 60Fat | 5g Protein |4g   Carbs| 8g Fibre| 1.6g

Ingredients:

- 1 bunch of kale, with the stems removed and torn into bite-sized pieces
- 15 ml (1 heap tablespoon) of extra virgin olive oil
- 15 grams (1 tablespoon of Za'atar seasoning
- 1 grain (1 pinch of salt)

Directions:

1. Preheat your air fryer to a temperature of 190°C (375°F).
2. In a deep bowl, toss all together the kale with the olive oil, the Za'atar seasoning, and the salt.
3. Place the kale in your air fryer basket in one single layer.
4. Air fry the kale for about 5 to 7 minutes, shaking the basket every few minutes, until the edges become slightly brown and the kale becomes crispy.
5. Remove the kale chips from your air fryer and let them cool for a few minutes before serving.
6. Enjoy your delicious vegan Za'atar kale chips!

PLANT BASED VEGAN AIR FRYER MAIN RECIPES

41. EGGPLANT VEGAN PASTA

Servings| 4 Time|15 minutes
Nutritional Content (per serving):
Cal | 399 Fat | 15g Protein |12.3g Carbs| 13g Fibre| 1.7g

Ingredients:

- 1 large sliced into rounds of 1/4 inch each of the eggplant slices
- 200 grams (1 cup) of all-purpose flour
- 30 grams (2 tablespoons) of nutritional yeast
- 8 grams (1 teaspoon) of garlic powder
- 8 grams (1 teaspoon) of onion powder
- 4 grams (1/2 teaspoon) of salt

- 2 grams (1/4 teaspoon) of black pepper
- 200 grams (1 cup) of panko bread crumbs
- 50 ml (1/4 cup) of almond milk (e.g. soy milk)
- 15 ml (1 tablespoon) of apple cider vinegar
- 15 ml (1 heap) tablespoon of extra virgin olive oil
- 250 ml (1 cup) of marinara sauce
- 100 grams (1/2 cup) of vegan shredded mozzarella cheese
- 30 grams (2 tablespoons) of fresh basil leaves, for garnish (optional)

Ingredients for Pasta:

- 250 grams (8 oz) of your preferred pasta (e.g. spaghetti, linguine, or penne)
- 1 grain (1 pinch) of salt, for cooking the pasta

Directions:

1. Preheat your air fryer to a temperature of about 175°C (390°F).
2. In a shallow bowl, whisk together the all-purpose flour, the nutritional yeast, the garlic powder, the onion powder, salt, and black pepper.
3. In another shallow bowl, mix the panko breadcrumbs with the plant-based milk, apple cider vinegar, and olive oil. Stir until the mixture resembles coarse sand.
4. Dip each eggplant slice into the flour mixture, shaking off any excess. Then, dip each slice into the panko mixture, pressing the crumbs onto the eggplant to make sure they adhere.

5. Place the coated eggplant slices in the air fryer basket, making sure they don't overlap. Air fry for about 8 to 10 minutes, or until the eggplant slices become golden brown and crispy in color
6. While the eggplant is cooking, cook the pasta according to the package instructions. Drain and set aside.
7. When the eggplant is done, remove it from the air fryer and place it on a serving platter.
8. Spoon the marinara sauce over the eggplant slices and sprinkle the vegan shredded mozzarella cheese on top.
9. Place the platter back in your air fryer and air fry for about 2 to3 minutes, or until the cheese is melted.
10. Serve the eggplant parmesan with the cooked pasta and garnish with fresh basil leaves, if desired. Enjoy!

42. AIR FRYER VEGAN BEAN BURGERS

Servings| 4 Time|15 minutes

Nutritional Content (per serving):

Cal |320 Fat | 11.3g Protein |11.2g Carbs| 13.4g Fibre| 2g

Ingredients:

- 1 can, of 450 grams (1 pound) of black beans, drained and rinsed
- 100 grams (1/2 cup) of oats
- 100 grams (1/2 cup) of bread crumbs
- ½ cup, 1/2 red onion, finely chopped
- 1 garlic clove, finely minced
- 15 grams (1 tablespoon) of ground flaxseed
- 15 ml (1 tablespoon) of water
- 15 ml (1 tablespoon) of soy sauce
- 15 grams (1 tablespoon) of nutritional yeast

- 1 grain (1 pinch) of paprika
- 15 milliliters (1tablespoon) of cooking spray
- 1 grain (1 pinch) of salt
- 1/2 teaspoon of cumin
- 1 grain (1 pinch) of ground black pepper

Directions:

1. Preheat your air fryer to a temperature of about 175°C (390°F).
2. In a food processor, pulse the oats until they become a fine flour-like texture.
3. In a small bowl, mix the ground flaxseed with water and let it sit for a few minutes to thicken.
4. In a large mixing bowl, mash the black beans with a fork or a potato masher until they become a chunky paste.
5. Add the oat flour, breadcrumbs, red onion, garlic, soy sauce, nutritional yeast, smoked paprika, cumin, salt, black pepper, and flaxseed mixture to the bowl with the mashed black beans. Mix everything together until well combined.
6. Divide the mixture into 4-6 portions and form each portion into a patty shape.
7. Spray your air fryer basket with the cooking spray and arrange your patties in the basket. Make sure they don't overlap.
8. Air fry the patties for 10-12 minutes, flipping halfway through, or until they are crispy on the outside and heated through.
9. Serve the black bean burgers on a bun with your favorite toppings, such as avocado, tomato, lettuce, or vegan mayo.
10. Enjoy your air fryer vegan black bean burgers!

43.   AIR FRYER VEGAN QUORN VEGAN FILLETS WITH RICE

Servings| 4 Time|15 minutes

Nutritional Content (per serving):

Cal | 365Fat | 10g Protein |7.3g   Carbs| 13g Fibre| 1.5g

Ingredients:

- ❖ 2 Quorn Vegan Fillets
- ❖ 200 grams (1 cup) of brown rice
- ❖ 500 ml (2 cups) of water
- ❖ 1 gain (1 pinch) of salt
- ❖ 1 grain (1 pinch) of ground black pepper

- ❖ 4 grams (1/2 teaspoon) of garlic powder
- ❖ 4 grams (1/2 teaspoon) of onion powder
- ❖ 4 grams (1/2 teaspoon) of paprika
- ❖ 15 ml (1 heap tablespoon) of vegetable olive oil
- ❖ Optional: 100 grams of sliced vegetables (such as bell pepper, onion, and zucchini)

Directions:

1. Preheat your air fryer to a temperature of about 200°C (400°F).
2. Rinse the brown rice and add it to a pot with 2 cups of water, salt, and black pepper. Bring to a boil, then reduce heat to low, cover, and let simmer for 40-45 minutes, or until the water is absorbed and the rice is tender.
3. In a small bowl, mix the garlic powder, onion powder, paprika, and olive oil.
4. Brush the Quorn Vegan Fillets with the seasoning mixture, making sure to cover all sides.
5. If you're using sliced vegetables, add them to your air fryer basket along with the seasoned fillets.
6. Place the fillets and the vegetables (if using) in your air fryer basket and cook for about 12-15 minutes, flipping the fillets halfway through, until they're golden brown and crispy.
7. Serve the fillets and vegetables over a bed of rice and enjoy!

44. VEGAN PLANT BASED FAJITAS

Servings| 4-6Time|12 minutes

Nutritional Content (per serving):

Cal | 266Fat | 8.5g Protein |9g Carbs| 13.6g Fibre| 1.7g

Ingredients:

- ❖ 4 to 6 tortillas
- ❖ 1 red bell pepper, finely sliced
- ❖ 1 green bell pepper, sliced
- ❖ 1 finely sliced onion
- ❖ 15 ml (1 heap tablespoon) of vegetable or extra virgin olive oil

- ❖ 8 grams (1 teaspoon) of chili powder
- ❖ 8 grams (1 teaspoon) of ground cumin
- ❖ 4 grams (1/2 teaspoon) of garlic powder
- ❖ 1 grain (1 pinch) of salt
- ❖ 1 grain (1 pinch) of ground black pepper

Directions:

1. Preheat your air fryer to a temperature of about 175°C (390°F).
2. In a bowl, mix all together the sliced bell peppers with the onion, olive oil, chili powder, cumin, garlic powder, salt, and pepper until well combined.
3. Transfer the mixture to your air fryer basket and cook for about 10 to 12 minutes, shaking the basket occasionally, until the vegetables are tender and slightly charred.
4. Warm the tortillas in the microwave or on a griddle.
5. Assemble the fajitas by placing a few spoonfuls of the vegetable mixture onto a warm tortilla.
6. Add any additional toppings you like, such as avocado, salsa, or vegan sour cream.
7. Fold the tortilla and enjoy your dish!

➢ **Note:** Cooking times may vary depending on your air fryer model, so keep an eye on the vegetables while they cook. You can also adjust the seasonings to your taste.

45.   PLANT BASED VEGAN PULLED PORK

Servings| 4Time|20minutes
Nutritional Content (per serving):
Cal | 330Fat | 8g Protein |9g   Carbs| 18g Fibre| 2g

Ingredients:

- ❖ 1 can young jackfruit in water or brine (not syrup) 450 grams (1 pound)
- ❖ 1/2 onion, chopped
- ❖ 2 garlic cloves, minced
- ❖ 1 tablespoon olive oil
- ❖ 1 teaspoon smoked paprika
- ❖ 1 teaspoon cumin

- ❖ 1/2 teaspoon salt
- ❖ 1/4 teaspoon black pepper
- ❖ 1/4 cup apple cider vinegar
- ❖ 1/4 cup low-sugar or sugar-free barbecue sauce
- ❖ 1/4 cup water

Directions:

1. Start by preheating your air fryer to a temperature of 375°F (190°C).
2. Drain the jackfruit and rinse it very well with water. Make sure to squeeze out any excess water and pat dry with the help of a clean towel.
3. Heat the olive oil in a skillet over a medium heat; then add in the onion and the garlic and cook until everything is very well softened.
4. Add in the jackfruit to your skillet and cook for about 5 minutes, making sure to stir occasionally.
5. Add the smoked paprika, the cumin, the salt, and the ground black pepper to the skillet and stir to combine.
6. Add in the apple cider vinegar, barbecue sauce, and water to the skillet and stir to combine.
7. Transfer the jackfruit mixture to your air fryer basket and cook for 12-15 minutes, or until the jackfruit is crispy on the outside.
8. Remove the basket from the air fryer and use a fork to shred the jackfruit into small pieces.
9. Serve the pulled jackfruit on a bun or in a lettuce wrap, topped with your favorite toppings. Enjoy!

46. AIR FRYER TOFU VEGGIE STIR FRY

Servings| 2-3Time|12 minutes
Nutritional Content (per serving):
Cal | 275Fat | 13g Protein |13g Carbs| 12.1g Fibre| 2g

Ingredients:

❖ 1 block of firm tofu
❖ 1 bell pepper, sliced
❖ 1 onion, sliced
❖ 1 zucchini, sliced
❖ 15 grams (tablespoon) of cornstarch

❖ 15 ml (1 tablespoon) of vegetable oil
❖ 15 ml (1 tablespoon) of soy sauce
❖ 1 grain (1 pinch) of salt
❖ 1 grain (1 pinch) of ground black pepper

Directions:

1. Start by preheating your air fryer to a temperature of about 175°C (390°F).
2. Press the tofu to remove excess water, and then cut it into small cubes.
3. In a bowl, mix the cubed tofu with soy sauce and cornstarch, making sure all pieces are well coated.
4. Place the tofu in the air fryer basket and cook for 10 minutes, flipping the tofu pieces halfway through the cooking time.
5. While the tofu is cooking, heat the oil in a pan over medium-high heat. Add the sliced bell pepper, onion, and zucchini and sauté until they are tender.
6. Once the tofu is done cooking in the air fryer, add it to the pan with the sautéed vegetables and stir everything together.
7. Season with salt and pepper to taste and cook for an additional 1-2 minutes until everything is heated through.
8. Serve and enjoy your vegan tofu veggie stir fry!

➢ **Note:** You can customize this recipe by using different vegetables, such as broccoli, carrots, or mushrooms. You can also adjust the seasoning to your taste.

47.   VEGAN CAULIFLOWER TACOS

Servings|3-4 Time|12 minutes
Nutritional Content (per serving):
Cal |302Fat |6g Protein |6.3g Carbs| 10g Fibre| 1.3 g

Ingredients:

- ❖ 1 head of cauliflower, cut into small florets
- ❖ 15 ml (1 tablespoon) of vegetable or extra virgin olive oil
- ❖ 15 grams (1 tablespoon) of chili powder
- ❖ 8 grams (1 teaspoon) of ground cumin
- ❖ 8 grams (1 teaspoon) of garlic powder

- ❖ 8-10 small corn tortillas
- ❖ Toppings (optional): avocado, salsa, chopped cilantro, diced onion, lime wedges
- ❖ 1 grain (1 pinch) of salt
- ❖ 1 grain (1 pinch) of ground black pepper

Directions:

1. Start by preheating your air fryer to a temperature of about 175°C (390°F).
2. In a bowl, combine the cauliflower florets with olive oil, chili powder, cumin, garlic powder, salt, and black pepper. Mix until the cauliflower is evenly coated.
3. Place the seasoned cauliflower in your air fryer basket and cook for about 10-12 minutes, shaking the basket every few minutes to ensure even cooking. The cauliflower should be tender and slightly crispy when done.
4. Warm the corn tortillas in the microwave or on a griddle.
5. To assemble the tacos, add a spoonful of the cooked cauliflower to each tortilla, and top with your desired toppings such as avocado, salsa, cilantro, onion, and lime wedges.
6. Serve and enjoy your vegan cauliflower tacos!

> **Note:** You can also experiment with different seasonings for the cauliflower, such as smoked paprika, oregano, or chipotle powder. Feel free to adjust the toppings to your liking.

48.   VEGAN AIR FRYER MUSHROOM BURGERS

Servings|2Time|10 minutes

Nutritional Content (per serving):

Cal |115Fat |10g Protein |8.5g   Carbs| 9.3g Fibre| 1.6 g

Ingredients:

- 4 large Portobello mushroom caps
- 15 ml (1 tablespoon) of vegetable or olive oil
- 15 ml (1 tablespoon) of balsamic vinegar
- 8 grams (1 teaspoon) of garlic powder

- 4 burger buns
- Toppings (optional): lettuce, tomato, onion, avocado, vegan mayo
- 1grain (1 pinch) of salt
- 1grain (1 pinch) of ground black pepper

Directions:

1. Preheat your air fryer to a temperature of about 175°C (390°F).
2. Gently clean the Portobello mushroom caps with a damp paper towel, removing any dirt. Remove the stems and gills.
3. In a large and deep bowl, whisk together the olive oil, the balsamic vinegar, garlic powder, salt, and pepper. Brush the mixture onto both sides of the mushroom caps
4. Place the mushroom caps in your air fryer basket and cook for about 8 to 10 minutes, flipping them halfway through the cooking time.
5. While the mushrooms are cooking, prepare the toppings and toast the burger buns.
6. To assemble the burgers, place a cooked mushroom cap on each bun, and add your desired toppings such as lettuce, tomato, onion, avocado, and vegan mayo.
7. Serve and enjoy your vegan air fryer mushroom burgers!

➢ **Note:** You can also experiment with different seasonings for the mushrooms, such as smoked paprika, thyme, or rosemary. Feel free to adjust the toppings to your liking.

49. PLANT BASED VEGAN AIR FRYER RATATOUILLE

Servings|3 Time|6 minutes

Nutritional Content (per serving):

Cal |286Fat |11.3g Protein |9.8g Carbs| 12g Fibre| 1.6 g

Ingredients:

- ❖ 1 large eggplant, cubed
- ❖ 1 large zucchini, cubed
- ❖ 1 large red bell pepper, seeded and cubed
- ❖ 1 large yellow onion, diced
- ❖ 3 cloves of garlic, minced
- ❖ 30 ml (2 tablespoons) of olive oil

- ❖ 15 grams (1 tablespoon) of dried thyme
- ❖ 15 grams (1 tablespoon) of dried rosemary
- ❖ 1grain (1 pinch) of salt
- ❖ 1grain (1 pinch) of ground black pepper
- ❖ 1 can of 450 grams (14 oz) of diced tomatoes, drained

Directions:

1. Start by preheating your air fryer to a temperature of about 175°C (390°F).
2. In a large deep bowl, combine all together the cubed eggplant, the zucchini, and the red bell pepper. Add in the olive oil and toss to coat the vegetables.
3. Spread your vegetables in one single layer in your air fryer basket. Cook for about 12-15 minutes, shaking the basket occasionally, until the vegetables are tender and slightly browned.
4. While the vegetables are cooking, heat 15 ml (1 tablespoon) of vegetable or olive oil in a large pan over medium-high heat. Add the diced onion and garlic and sauté for 2-3 minutes until softened.
5. Add the cooked vegetables to the pan with the onion and garlic. Add the dried thyme and rosemary, and season with salt and pepper to taste.
6. Add the drained diced tomatoes to the pan and stir everything together.
7. Cook for an additional 2-3 minutes, until the flavors are well combined and the ratatouille is heated through.
8. Serve and enjoy your vegan air fryer ratatouille!

> **Note:** Ratatouille is a versatile dish, so feel free to customize it with your favorite vegetables and herbs. You can also add a splash of balsamic vinegar or lemon juice for extra flavor.

50. VEGAN RICE BALLS WITH SAUCE

Servings|4 Time|12 minutes

Nutritional Content (per serving):

Cal |265Fat |8.6g Protein |13g   Carbs| 15g Fibre| 1 g

Ingredients:

- 400 grams (1 pound) of cooked white rice
- 100 grams (1/2 cup) of vegan shredded mozzarella cheese
- 100 grams (1/2 cup) of finely chopped spinach
- 100 grams (1/4 cup) of finely chopped sun-dried tomatoes
- 50 grams (1/4 cup) of finely chopped Kalamata olives
- 50 grams (1/4 cup) of vegan bread crumbs
- 15 grams (1 tablespoon) of dried oregano
- 8 grams (1 teaspoon) of garlic powder
- 1grain (1 pinch) of salt
- 1grain (1 pinch) of ground black pepper

Directions:

1. In a large deep bowl, combine the cooked white rice, the vegan shredded mozzarella cheese, chopped spinach, sun-dried tomatoes, Kalamata olives, vegan breadcrumbs, dried oregano, garlic powder, salt, and pepper. Mix well.
2. Using your hands, form the mixture into small balls, about 1-2 inches in diameter.
3. Preheat your air fryer to a temperature of about 175°C (390°F).
4. Place the rice balls in your air fryer basket, making sure they are not touching each other.
5. Cook your rice balls for about 10 to 12 minutes, shaking your basket occasionally, until they are golden brown and crispy.
6. Serve your vegan air fryer rice balls with your favorite dipping sauce, such as marinara sauce or vegan aioli.

> **Note:** You can also experiment with different fillings for the rice balls, such as diced mushrooms, roasted red peppers, or vegan sausage crumbles. You can also use leftover rice from a previous meal to make this recipe even easier.

51.   VEGAN POTATO CURRY

Servings|4 Time|10 minutes

Nutritional Content (per serving):

Cal |322Fat |11g Protein |12.1g   Carbs| 16g Fibre| 2g

Ingredients:

- 4 large carrots, 250 grams (½ pound)
- 2 large potatoes, 250 grams (1/2 pound)
- 8 ml (1 teaspoon) of maple syrup
- 16 grams (2 teaspoons) of curry
- 1 sprig of thyme
- 1 clove of garlic

- 15ml (1 tablespoon) of vegetable or extra virgin olive oil
- 1grain (1 pinch) of salt
- 1grain (1 pinch) of ground black pepper

Directions:

1. Peel and wash the carrots, cut them into slices of about 5 millimeters. Pour the carrots into a bowl. Add a drizzle of extra virgin olive oil, maple syrup, curry and thyme.
2. Stir with a spoon to combine the ingredients.
3. Pour the carrots into the air fryer basket lined with parchment paper (better the one with holes for the air fryer). Cook in an air fryer, possibly preheated, at 180° C (360°F) for 10 minutes.
4. Meanwhile, peel and wash the potatoes. Then, cut them into thin slices (like crisps). Pour them into the bowl where the carrots were flavored; mix with a spoon.
5. Also add the garlic clove and continue cooking in the air fryer for another 10 minutes or until the vegetables are golden brown
6. Season with salt. Serve the carrots and potatoes with curry and maple syrup.
7. Enjoy your dish!

52. VEGAN BULGUR STEAKS

Servings|3-4 Time|20 minutes

Nutritional Content (per serving):

Cal |290Fat |10.5g Protein |11g   Carbs| 15.6 g Fibre| 2.1g

Ingredients:

- ❖ 100 grams (1/4 pound) of kasha
- ❖ 35grams (1/4 cup) of bulgur
- ❖ 1/2 onion
- ❖ 1 grain (1 pinch) of baking soda
- ❖ 15 grams (1 tablespoon) of flour
- ❖ A few parsley leaves
- ❖ 1 teaspoon (8ml) of soy sauce
- ❖ 1 large egg

- ❖ 15ml (1 tablespoon) of vegetable or extra virgin olive oil
- ❖ 1grain (1 pinch) of salt
- ❖ 1grain (1 pinch) of ground black pepper

Directions:

1. Start by peeling the onion and chopping it. Then sauté it for 5 minutes in a large pan with oil.
2. Add the bulgur and kasha. Mix; then add the sodium bicarbonate and cover with 250 ml (1 cup) of hot water,
3. At the first boil, cover the pan and leave to swell off the heat for 10 minutes,
4. In a salad bowl, mix the flour, the soy sauce, the chopped parsley then add the kasha and the drained bulgur,
5. Mix everything well,
6. Heat your Air fryer to a temperature of 190°C (380°F) with oil then pour the preparation so as to form two steaks.
7. Arrange in your Air Fryer basket.
8. Cook the steaks for about 10 minutes, 5 minutes on each side.
9. Serve and enjoy with a good green salad and a homemade vinaigrette.

53. VEGAN TORTILLAS

Servings|4 Time|10 minutes

Nutritional Content (per serving):

Cal |285Fat |11g Protein |9.3g Carbs| 14g Fibre| 1.8g

Ingredients:

For the marinated cabbage and red onion

- ❖ 250ml (1 cup) boiling water
- ❖ 250 ml (1 cup) white vinegar
- ❖ 80 ml (1/3 cup) of maple syrup or stevia
- ❖ 500 ml (2 cups) of finely shredded red cabbage
- ❖ 1/2 red onion, minced

For the avocado cream

- ❖ 2 ½ ml (1/2 teaspoon) of ground cumin
- ❖ 5 ml (1/2 teaspoon) of ground cilantro
- ❖ ½ tsp (5 ml) of chili powder
- ❖ 1 clove garlic, minced
- ❖ 375 ml (1 1/2 cups) of finely chopped walnuts
- ❖ 1 grain (1 pinch) of salt
- ❖ 1 grain (1 pinch) of ground black pepper
- ❖ 12 gluten-free corn tortillas

- ❖ 1 avocado
- ❖ 60 ml (1/4 cup) of vegetable mayonnaise
- ❖ The juice of 1/2 lime
- ❖ 250 ml (1 cup) of chopped fresh cilantro
- ❖ 1/2 jalapeno pepper, seeded, chopped
- ❖ 1.25 ml (1/4 tsp) of salt

For the cauliflower Tacos

- ❖ 750 ml (3 cups) of chopped cauliflower
- ❖ 1/2 red onion, chopped
- ❖ 45 ml (3 tablespoons) of vegetable or olive oil

Directions:

1. For the marinated cabbage and red onion
2. In a large bowl, pour boiling water, vinegar, and maple syrup and mix. Add the cabbage and onion.
3. In a narrow container using a blender, mix all the ingredients for the avocado cream until you obtain a smooth purée.
4. For the cauliflower Tacos, preheat your Air Fryer to a temperature of about 200°C (400°F)

5. Place the cauliflower and onion in your Air Fryer basket with a bit of oil; cook for about 7 minutes.
6. Add the rest of the ingredients, salt, and pepper. Air fry for another 2 additional minutes, making sure to mix very well.
7. Wrap the tortillas in aluminum foil and warm them for 5 minutes.
8. Top the tortillas with the mixture of cauliflower, avocado cream and marinated cabbage and red onion.

54. VEGAN AIR FRYER PASTA

Servings|2-4 Time|12 minutes

Nutritional Content (per serving):

Cal |312Fat |12g Protein |8g   Carbs| 13.5g Fibre| 1g

Ingredients:

For Cooking Pasta:
❖   450 grams (1 pound) of short pasta (rigatoni, penne or farfalle)

For The Seasoning
❖   60 ml (1/4 cup) of vegetable or olive oil - 60 ml (¼ cup)
❖   60 ml (¼ cup) Nutritional yeast
❖   60 ml (1/4 cup) of Panko breadcrumbs (or other breadcrumbs of your choice)

❖ ❖   1grain (1 pinch) of salt
❖   1grain (1 pinch) of ground black pepper
❖   30 grams (2 tablespoons) of cornstarch
❖   10 grams (2 teaspoons) of dried Italian herbs
❖   5 grams (1 teaspoon) of garlic powder
❖   5 grams (1 teaspoon) of hot pepper flakes
❖   1 grain (1 pinch) of salt

Directions:

1. Cook the pasta in boiling salted water for 1 minute less than indicated on the package (al dente).
2. Drain the pasta, but do not rinse it. Return the cooked pasta to the cauldron or bowl.
3. Add the oil, nutritional yeast, breadcrumbs, cornstarch, and spices to the cooked pasta. Mix everything.
4. Put the seasoned pasta in the basket of your Air fryer, avoiding overloading the appliance so that the air circulates (you can do this in 2 or 3 batches).
5. Air fry for about 10 to 12 minutes at a temperature of 175° C (350° F), stirring halfway through cooking.
6. Reheat the marinara sauce or prepare any other dipping sauce of your choice.
7. Serve the sauce with the hot pasta.

55. VEGAN CAULIFLOWER WITH HARISSA SAUCE

Servings|4 Time|12 minutes

Nutritional Content (per serving):

Cal |268Fat |5g Protein |4.8g   Carbs| 12g Fibre| 1.5g

Ingredients:

- ❖ 1 medium cauliflower 450 grams (about 1 pound) in florets
- ❖ 45 grams (3 tablespoons) of harissa sweet sauce
- ❖ 30 ml (2 tablespoons) of vegetable or extra virgin olive oil
- ❖ 30 ml (2 tablespoons) of stevia
- ❖ 60 grams (¼ cup) flat-leaf parsley for garnish

Directions:

1. Cut the cauliflower into florets.
2. In a large bowl, add the harissa sauce, olive oil and maple syrup. Mix well to combine everything.
3. Add the cauliflower florets to the bowl and using a spoon or your hands stir the cauliflower florets to distribute the sauce evenly over all the florets.
4. Place the florets in the baskets of the Air Fryer in a single layer, so you will need to cook them in two batches.
5. Bake at 195° C (390 F°) for 12 minutes, turning every 4 minutes.
6. Serve hot garnished with parsley.
7. Enjoy your dish!

56. VEGAN POTATOES AND CHICKPEAS

Servings|4Time|35minutes

Nutritional Content (per serving):

Cal |186Fat |7g Protein |12g   Carbs| 13g Fibre| 1.6g

Ingredients:

- 900 grams (2 pounds) of potatoes, peeled and cut into 1.5cm/½in cubes
- small head of cauliflower, cut into florets (about 3 cups)
- 1 box chickpeas 450 grams (1 pound), rinsed and drained

- 45 ml (3 tablespoons) of vegetable olive oil
- 10 grams (2 teaspoons) curry powder
- 1 grain (1 pinch) of salt
- 1 grain (1 pinch) of ground black pepper
- 45 grams (3 tablespoons) of cilantro or fresh parsley, finely chopped

Directions:

1. Preheat your air fryer to a temperature of about 200° C (400° F).
2. Place potatoes, the cauliflower, the chickpeas, the olive oil, the curry powder, and the salt in a large bowl
3. Toss your ingredients very well to coat, season with ground black pepper.
4. Place your vegetables in your Air Fryer basket and drizzle with oil.
5. Air fry for about 30 to 35 minutes making sure to shake throughout the way.
6. Sprinkle with the cilantro
7. Serve and enjoy your dish!

57. VEGAN CHICKPEA BURGERS

Servings|2-4Time|12minutes

Nutritional Content (per serving):

Cal |313Fat |12g Protein |13.5g   Carbs| 18g Fibre| 1.7g

Ingredients:

for the burger dough:

- ❖ 200 g chickpeas for the peas
- ❖ 1/2 large, sweet onion
- ❖ 3 cloves of garlic
- ❖ 1 cup fresh cilantro (stems removed)
- ❖ 1 cup fresh parsley (stems removed)
- ❖ 8 grams (1 teaspoon) of cumin powder
- ❖ 15 grams (1 tablespoon) of baking soda
- ❖ 15 grams (1 tablespoon) of salt
- ❖ 1 grain (1 pinch) of freshly ground black pepper

for the vegan mayonnaise:

- ❖ 125grams (1/2 cup) of soy yoghurt
- ❖ 30 ml (2 tablespoons) of sunflower oil
- ❖ 1 clove of garlic
- ❖ 15 ml (1 tablespoon) of lemon juice
- ❖ 1 grain (1 pinch) of salt

Directions:

1. Clean the chickpeas and let them soak overnight.
2. Once the soaking time is over, drain the chickpeas and mix them with all the ingredients.
3. Divide the dough into 4 equal portions. Form a ball with each portion and flatten it into a hamburger shape.
4. Place the burgers in the 6-liter fryer tray and add half a tablespoon of oil.
5. Place the tray in the fryer; and air fry for about 12 minutes. After about 6 minutes, open the fryer, flip the burgers, and close it.
6. To make the vegan yogurt mayonnaise, whisk in the soy yogurt and gradually add the sunflower oil in a thin stream, whisking until emulsified. Add 1 tablespoon of lemon juice, 1 garlic and salt to taste, and whisk a little more.
7. You can garnish your burger with a pickle for an exquisite touch.
8. Enjoy your dish!

58. VEGAN TOFU TACOS

Servings|4Time|10 minutes

Nutritional Content (per serving):

Cal |313Fat |12g Protein |13.7g   Carbs| 18g Fibre| 1.7g

Ingredients:

- ❖ 1 Block of 450grams (1 pound) of firm tofu, rinsed and patted dry

For the quick tandoori paste
- ❖ 15 grams (1 tablespoon) of garam masala
- ❖ 4 grams (1/2 teaspoon) of paprika
- ❖ 4 grams (1/2 teaspoon) of turmeric
- ❖ 4 grams (1/2 teaspoon) of ground ginger
- ❖ 2 grams (1/4 teaspoon) of garlic powder
- ❖ 1 grain (1 pinch) of cayenne

- ❖ The juice of half a lemon
- ❖ 8 grams (1/2 tablespoon) of tomato paste
- ❖ 30 ml (2 tablespoons) of stevia
- ❖ 1 grain (1 pinch) of salt
- ❖ 1 grain (1 pinch) of ground black pepper, to taste

For the tzatziki sauce
- ❖ 175 ml (1/2 cup) of plain soy yogurt
- ❖ 100 grams (½ cup) of cucumber, finely grated
- ❖ 30 grams (2 tablespoons) of chopped cilantro or mint
- ❖ The juice of half a lime
- ❖ 1 grain (1 pinch) of salt
- ❖ 1 grain (1 pinch) of ground black pepper, to taste

For assembly
- ❖ 12 plain square naan buns, 30grams each
- ❖ 4 Lebanese cucumbers, sliced lengthwise (like a ribbon)
- ❖ 30 grams (2 tablespoons) of chopped cilantro, to taste
- ❖ lime, quartered
- ❖ 1 avocado, sliced
- ❖ 8 cherry tomatoes, sliced

Directions:

1. For the quick tandoori paste, in a bowl, mix all the ingredients together. If the dough is too dense, add a little more olive oil or water if necessary and set aside.
2. Cut the tofu into several sticks about 1.5 cm wide.
3. Using a pastry brush, brush the tofu sticks with the tandoori paste.
4. Reserve the tofu in the refrigerator for a minimum of four hours.
5. Place the tofu sticks in the basket of the air fryer, cook for 5 minutes at 200°C (400°F).
6. Flip the tofu sticks and continue cooking for 5 minutes at the same temperature.

For the tzatziki sauce:

7. In a bowl, mix all the ingredients together and reserve in the refrigerator.

For assembly:

8. Reheat the naan bread for 1 minute in the air fryer at 375 F.
9. Garnish the naan bread with tzatziki sauce, tofu sticks, sliced cucumber, tomatoes, and cilantro.
10. Add a little lime juice to taste. Serve and enjoy your tacos!

59. VEGAN ZUCCHINI GRATIN

Servings|2-4Time|15minutes

Nutritional Content (per serving):

Cal |289Fat |12g Protein |10.1g Carbs| 12g Fibre| 1.5 g

Ingredients:

* 2 zucchini, 250 grams (1/2 pound)
* 15 grams (1 tablespoon) of chopped fresh parsley.
* 30 grams (2 tablespoons) of breadcrumbs

* 4 tablespoons (1/2 cup) grated cashew cheese
* 15 ml (1 tablespoon) of vegetable oil
* 1 grain (1 pinch) of ground black pepper

Directions:

1. Preheat your Air fryer to 180° C (360°F).
2. Cut the zucchini in half, lengthwise, then divide each piece down the middle again. You get 8 pieces of zucchini. Place them in the basket of the Air fryer.
3. Mix the parsley, breadcrumbs, cheese, oil and freshly ground black pepper.
4. Fill the zucchini with the mixture. Slide the basket into the Air fryer and set the timer for 15 minutes.
5. Air fry the zucchini gratin until the timer rings and the gratin is golden brown.

60.   VEGAN CAULIFLOWER SAUTÉ

Servings|4Time|20minutes

Nutritional Content (per serving):

Cal |156Fat |11g Protein |13.5g   Carbs| 10g Fibre| 1.3 g

Ingredients:

- 1 head of cauliflower, cut into small pieces
- 100 grams (1/2 cup) all-purpose flour
- 1 teaspoon smoked paprika
- 4 grams (1/2 teaspoon) of garlic powder
- 4 grams (1/2 teaspoon) of salt

- 1 grain (1 pinch) of ground black pepper
- 125 ml (1/2 cup) unsweetened almond milk
- 200 grams (1 cup) panko breadcrumbs
- 15 ml (1 tablespoon) of olive oil spray

Directions:

1. Preheat the Air fryer to 200° C (400°F)
2. In a large bowl, combine the flour, paprika, garlic powder, salt, and black pepper.
3. Slowly add the almond milk while stirring until well incorporated.
4. Add the cauliflower to the bowl and toss well to coat each piece.
5. Add the panko breadcrumbs to another bowl.
6. Take each piece of coated cauliflower and roll it in panko breadcrumbs to completely cover it.
7. Place the coated cauliflower pieces on a baking sheet lined with parchment paper.
8. Lightly spray the cauliflower pieces with olive oil spray.
9. Place the baking sheet in the air fryer and bake for 15-20 minutes until the cauliflower is golden brown and crispy.
10. Remove baking sheet from air fryer and serve immediately.
11. Enjoy your dish!

Air Fryer Whole Vegan Sides and Salads

61.   VEGAN SPICY TOFU SALAD

Servings|3-4Time|12 minutes

Nutritional Content (per serving):

Cal |175Fat |11g Protein |13.2g   Carbs| 13g Fibre| 1.2 g

Ingredients:

- ❖ 400grams (1 pound) of firm tofu
- ❖ 2 tablespoons (30 grams) of cornstarch
- ❖ 1 tablespoon (15grams) of paprika
- ❖ 1 tablespoon (15 grams) of garlic powder
- ❖ 1 tablespoon (15 grams) of onion powder
- ❖ 1 tablespoon (15 grams) of salt

- ❖ 1/2 tbsp (8 grams) of black pepper
- ❖ 1/4 cup (60 ml) of almond milk
- ❖ 2 cups (400 grams) of fresh vegetables of your choice (lettuce, spinach, grated carrots, cucumbers, etc.)
- ❖ 1/4 cup (60 ml) of salad dressing of your choice (olive oil vinaigrette, balsamic vinaigrette, lemon vinaigrette, etc.)

Directions:

1. Preheat the Air fryer to 200° C (400°F).
2. Cut the tofu into small cubes.
3. In a bowl, combine the cornstarch, paprika, garlic powder, onion powder, salt, and black pepper.
4. Add the almond milk to the dry mixture and stir until you get a thick paste.
5. Add the tofu cubes to the batter and stir until well coated.
6. Carefully place the tofu cubes in one single layer in your air fryer.
7. Cook for 10 to 12 minutes, stirring occasionally, until the tofu cubes are golden brown and crispy.
8. While the tofu cooks, prepare the vegetables and dressing.
9. In a large bowl, arrange the fresh vegetables.
10. Add the vinaigrette of your choice and mix well.
11. Once the tofu is cooked, add it to the salad and mix gently.
    Serve immediately and enjoy your salad!

62. WHOLE VEGAN SWEET POTATO ROLLS

Servings|4Time|12 minutes

Nutritional Content (per serving):

Cal |286Fat |13g Protein |14g   Carbs| 16g Fibre| 1.3 g

Ingredients:

* 2 medium, 250 grams (about ½ pound) of sweet potatoes
* 15 ml (1 tablespoon) of vegetable or olive oil
* 8 grams (1/2 tablespoon) of paprika
* 8 grams (1/2 tbsp) of garlic powder
* 8 grams (1/2 tablespoon) of salt

* 1 grain (1 pinch) of ground black pepper
* 6 sheets of spring roll pastry
* 100 grams (1/2 cup) of bean sprouts
* 100 grams (1/2 cup) grated carrots
* 100 grams (1/2 cup) shredded red cabbage
* 60 ml (1/4 cup) vegan hot sauce (optional)

Directions:

1. Start by preheating your air fryer to a temperature of about 200° C (400°F)
2. Carefully peel your sweet potatoes; then cut them into small cubes.
3. In a large bowl, combine the olive oil, paprika, garlic powder, salt, and black pepper.
4. Add the sweet potato cubes to the seasoning mixture and toss well to coat.
5. Place the sweet potato cubes in one single layer in your air fryer.
6. Cook for 10 to 12 minutes, stirring occasionally, until the sweet potato cubes are tender and golden brown.
7. While the sweet potatoes are cooking, prepare the ingredients for the spring rolls.
8. In a large bowl, combine bean sprouts, grated carrots, and shredded red cabbage.
9. Dip a sheet of spring roll pastry in hot water for about 10 seconds, until soft and easy to handle.
10. Place the sheet of spring roll dough on a clean, dry work surface.
11. Add a spoonful of cooked sweet potatoes and a small amount of the vegetable mixture to the center of the sheet.
12. Roll the spring roll pastry sheet tightly around the filling, folding the sides inward to form a roll.
13. Repeat steps 9-12 for the remaining spring roll pastry sheets.
14. Serve the vegan air fryer sweet potato rolls with the vegan hot sauce (optional) and enjoy!

63. VEGAN AIR FRYER CRUNCHY SALAD

Servings|4-6Time|5 minutes

Nutritional Content (per serving):

Cal |256Fat |10.8g Protein |9g   Carbs| 18g Fibre| 1.6 g

Ingredients:

- ❖ 400 grams (1 pound) of finely chopped red cabbage
- ❖ 400 grams (1 pound) of finely chopped kale
- ❖ 100 grams (1/2 cup) of grated carrots
- ❖ 100 grams (1/2 cup) of sliced radishes
- ❖ 50 grams (1/4 cup) of chopped red onion
- ❖ 50 grams (1/4 cup) of chopped fresh parsley
- ❖ 50 grams (1/4 cup) of sliced almonds

For the dressing:
- ❖ 30 ml (2 tablespoons) of apple cider vinegar
- ❖ 30 ml (2 tablespoons) of vegetable or olive oil
- ❖ 15 ml (1 tablespoon) of sugar substitute, like maple syrup
- ❖ 15 ml (1 tablespoon) of Dijon mustard
- ❖ 1 grain (1 pinch) of salt
- ❖ 1 grain (1 pinch) of freshly ground black pepper

Directions:

1. Preheat your air fryer to 180° C (360°F).
2. In a large bowl, combine the red cabbage, kale, shredded carrots, radishes, red onion and parsley.
3. In a small bowl, combine the apple cider vinegar, olive oil, maple syrup, Dijon mustard, salt, and pepper for the dressing.
4. Add the dressing to the salad and toss well to coat all the vegetables.
5. Spread the sliced almonds on a baking sheet and cook in the air fryer for 3-4 minutes, until golden and crispy.
6. Remove the almonds from the air fryer and let them cool slightly.
7. Add the crispy almonds to the salad just before serving.
8. Serve the Vegan Crispy Air Fried Salad immediately.
9. Enjoy your salad!

64. VEGAN AIR FRYER SPINACH SALAD

Servings|4Time|5 minutes

Nutritional Content (per serving):

Cal |270Fat |11g Protein |13g Carbs| 14g Fibre| 2.6 g

Ingredients:

- ❖ 400 grams (1 pound) of fresh spinach leaves
- ❖ 50 grams (1/4 cup) of raw cashews
- ❖ 50 grams (1/4 cup) of sunflower seeds
- ❖ 50 grams (1/4 cup) of raisins

- ❖ 50 grams (1/4 cup) chopped red onion
- ❖ 30 ml (2 tablespoons) of vegetable or olive oil
- ❖ 15 ml (1 heap tablespoon) of apple cider vinegar
- ❖ 15 ml (1 heap tablespoon) of fresh lemon juice
- ❖ 1 grain (1 pinch) of salt
- ❖ 1 grain (1 pinch) of freshly ground black pepper

Directions:

1. Preheat your air fryer to 180° C (360°F)
2. In a large bowl, combine the spinach leaves, cashews, sunflower seeds, raisins, and red onion.
3. In a small bowl, combine the olive oil, apple cider vinegar, lemon juice, salt, and pepper for the dressing.
4. Add the dressing to the salad and toss well to coat all the ingredients.
5. Spread the salad on a baking sheet and cook in the air fryer for 3 to 5 minutes, until the spinach leaves are slightly crispy.
6. Remove the salad from the air fryer and let it cool slightly.
7. Serve the sugar-free vegan spinach salad immediately, garnished with a few extra cashews and sunflower seeds if desired.
8. Enjoy your salad!

65. VEGAN AIR FRYER EGGPLANT SALAD

Servings|4Time|10 minutes

Nutritional Content (per serving):

Cal |185Fat |10g Protein |11g   Carbs| 11g Fibre| 2 g

Ingredients:

- ❖ 400 grams, 2 medium eggplants (about 1 pound)
- ❖ 30 ml (2 heap tablespoons) of olive oil
- ❖ 1 grain (1 pinch) of salt
- ❖ 1 grain (1 pinch) of ground black pepper
- ❖ 2 cloves of garlic, finely chopped
- ❖ 50 grams (1/4 cup) of chopped fresh basil leaves

- ❖ 50 grams (1/4 cup) of chopped fresh mint leaves
- ❖ 50 grams (1/4 cup) of roasted and chopped cashews

For the dressing:

- ❖ 30 ml (2 heap tablespoons) of olive oil
- ❖ 15 ml (1 heap tablespoon) of balsamic vinegar
- ❖ 8 ml (1 teaspoon) of sugar substitute, like maple syrup
- ❖ 1 grain (1 pinch) of salt
- ❖ 1 grain (1 pinch) of ground freshly ground black pepper

Directions:

1. Preheat your Air fryer to a temperature of 190° C (380°F).
2. Cut the eggplants into slices about no more than 1 cm thick.
3. Brush the eggplant slices with the olive oil and season with the salt and black pepper.
4. Place the eggplant rings in the air fryer in a single layer and cook for about 8-10 minutes, until golden brown and tender. Flip the eggplant slices halfway through cooking for even cooking.
5. Meanwhile, prepare the vinaigrette by mixing the olive oil, balsamic vinegar, maple syrup, salt, and black pepper.
6. In a large bowl, combine the cooked eggplant slices, minced garlic, fresh basil, fresh mint and toasted and chopped cashews.
7. Add the dressing to the salad and toss well to coat all the ingredients.
8. Serve the vegan eggplant salad immediately, garnished with additional basil and mint leaves if desired.

66.   VEGAN AIR FRYER TOFU VERMICELLI SALAD

Servings|4-6Time|8 minutes

Nutritional Content (per serving):

Cal |245Fat |12g Protein |10.8g   Carbs| 13g Fibre| 1.9 g

Ingredients:

- ❖ 8 sheets of rice
- ❖ 1 block of firm tofu, cut into strips
- ❖ 1/2 cucumber, cut into strips
- ❖ 1 peeled and finely cut into thin strips carrot

- ❖ 100 grams (about 1/2 cup) of red cabbage, thinly sliced
- ❖ 100 grams (about 1/2 cup) of fresh mint leaves
- ❖ 100 grams (1/2 cup) of fresh cilantro leaves
- ❖ 100 grams (1/2 cup) cooked rice vermicelli
- ❖ 250 l (1 cup) Peanut sauce for dipping

Directions:

1. Preheat the air fryer to 190° C (380°F).
2. Prepare all the ingredients and place them on a work surface.
3. Dip rice paper in lukewarm water for about 10 seconds or until softened.
4. Place the softened rice paper on a clean work surface and place a few strips of tofu, cucumber, carrot, as well as red cabbage, mint leaves, cilantro, and cooked rice vermicelli on the bottom part of the rice paper.
5. Fold the sides of the rice paper inward; then roll the rice paper tight, leaving the top open.
6. Repeat the process for the other rice papers and ingredients.
7. Lightly brush the spring rolls with olive oil.
8. Place the spring rolls in the air fryer in one single layer and cook for about 5-7 minutes, until golden brown and crispy.
9. Serve the vegan spring rolls immediately, along with peanut sauce for dipping.

67.   VEGAN AIR FRYER TOMATO CAPRESE SALAD

Servings|4Time|12 minutes

Nutritional Content (per serving):

Cal |87Fat |10g Protein |3g   Carbs| 10g Fibre| 1.3 g

Ingredients:

- 400 grams (1 pound) of caprese tomatoes
- 30 ml (2 heap tablespoons) of vegetable or olive oil

- 1 grain (1 pinch) of salt
- 1 grain (1 pinch) of ground black pepper
- 30 grams (2 tablespoons) of freshly chopped flat parsley

Directions:

1. Preheat your air fryer to 200° C (400°F)
2. Carefully wash your tomatoes and cut them into thin quarters.
3. In a bowl, combine the olive oil, salt and black pepper.
4. Add the tomato wedges to the bowl and toss to coat well in the olive oil.
5. Place the tomato wedges in your air fryer and cook for 10-12 minutes, stirring every few minutes, until golden brown and crispy.
6. Remove the tomato wedges from the air fryer and let them cool.
7. Sprinkle with the parsley; then serve and enjoy your salad!

68. VEGAN AIR FRYER BUTTON MUSHROOM SALAD

Servings|6Time|10 minutes

Nutritional Content (per serving):

Cal |103Fat |5.3g Protein |6g   Carbs| 11g Fibre| 1.2 g

Ingredients:

- ❖ 500 grams (1 pound) of button mushrooms
- ❖ 30 ml (2 heap tablespoons) of vegetable or olive oil
- ❖ 8 grams (1 teaspoon) garlic powder
- ❖ 1 grain (1 pinch) of salt

- ❖ 1 grain (1 pinch) of black pepper
- ❖ 400 grams (1 pound) of lettuce
- ❖ 50 grams (1/4 cup) of chopped walnuts
- ❖ 50 grams (1/4 cup) of cherry tomatoes, halved
- ❖ 1 small, diced cucumber

Directions:

1. Preheat your air fryer to 200° C (400°F).
2. Start by washing the mushrooms and cutting them into thin quarters.
3. In a bowl, combine the olive oil, garlic powder, salt, and black pepper.
4. Add the mushroom quarters to the bowl and toss to coat well in the olive oil.
5. Place the mushroom wedges in the air fryer and cook for 8 to 10 minutes, stirring every few minutes, until golden brown and crispy.
6. While the mushrooms cook, prepare the salad by arranging the mixed lettuce, walnuts, cherry tomatoes, and cucumber in a salad bowl.
7. Add the fried mushrooms to the salad and mix well.
8. Serve immediately and add a dressing of your choice if desired.
9. Enjoy your salad!

69.   VEGAN AIR FRYER GREEN BEAN SALAD

Servings|4Time|10 minutes

Nutritional Content (per serving):

Cal |96Fat |7.3g Protein |8.5g Carbs| 12.3g Fibre| 1.8 g

Ingredients:

- ❖ 500grams (1 pound) of fresh green beans
- ❖ 30 ml (2 heap tablespoons) of vegetable or olive oil
- ❖ 8 grams (1 teaspoon) of garlic powder
- ❖ 1 grain (1 pinch) of salt
- ❖ 1 grain (1 pinch) of ground black pepper

- ❖ 400 grams (1 pound) of cabbage, shredded
- ❖ 50 grams (1/4 cup) of chopped walnuts
- ❖ 100 grams (2 cups) of chopped fresh tomatoes
- ❖ 50 grams (1/4 cup) of finely chopped red onion
- ❖ 60 ml (1/4 cup) of balsamic vinaigrette

Directions:

1. Preheat your air fryer to 200° C (400°F).
2. Carefully wash; then cut the ends of the green beans.
3. In a bowl, combine the olive oil, garlic powder, salt, and black pepper.
4. Add the green beans to the bowl and toss them so they are well coated in the olive oil.
5. Place the green beans in your air fryer and air fry for 8-10 minutes, stirring every few minutes, until golden brown and crispy.
6. While the green beans are cooking, prepare the salad by mixing the shredded cabbage, walnuts, cherry tomatoes, and red onion in a salad bowl.
7. Add the air fried green beans to the salad and mix well.
8. Drizzle the balsamic vinaigrette over your salad and toss again.
9. Serve immediately and enjoy your salad.

70. VEGAN AIR FRYER LETTUCE AND CORN SALAD

Servings|4-6Time|10 minutes

Nutritional Content (per serving):

Cal |115Fat |6g Protein |9g   Carbs| 10g Fibre| 1.5 g

Ingredients:

- ❖ 200 grams (2 cups) of corn on the cob, shelled
- ❖ 1 red bell pepper, finely diced
- ❖ 1 green bell pepper, diced
- ❖ 1 small red onion, thinly sliced
- ❖ 30 ml (1 heap tablespoon) of olive oil
- ❖ 8 grams (1 teaspoon) of ground cumin
- ❖ 4 grams (1/2 teaspoon) of smoked paprika
- ❖ 1 grain (1 pinch) of salt
- ❖ 1 grain (1 pinch) of ground black pepper

For the salad:

- ❖ 400 grams (1 pound) of romaine lettuce
- ❖ 100 grams (1 heap cup) of black beans, rinsed and drained
- ❖ 1 avocado, diced
- ❖ 50 grams (1/4 cup) chopped fresh cilantro

For the dressing:

- ❖ 60 ml (1/4 cup) of fresh lime juice
- ❖ 30 ml (2 heap tablespoons) of vegetable or olive oil
- ❖ 1 clove of garlic, finely chopped
- ❖ 1/2 teaspoon of maple syrup
- ❖ 1 grain (1 pinch) of salt
- ❖ 1 grain (1 pinch) of ground black pepper

Directions:

1. Preheat your air fryer to 200° C. In a bowl, combine the corn, peppers, red onion, olive oil, cumin, smoked paprika, salt and black pepper.
2. Add the vegetable mixture to the air fryer and cook for 8-10 minutes, stirring every few minutes, until the vegetables are golden brown and crispy.
3. While the vegetables cook, prepare the salad by arranging the romaine lettuce, black beans, avocado and cilantro in a salad bowl. In a small bowl, combine all the dressing ingredients.
4. Pour the dressing over the salad and mix well.
5. Add the fried vegetables to the salad and mix again.

VEGAN AIR FRYER SNACKS

71. VEGAN AIR FRYER TOFU

Servings|4Time|12 minutes

Nutritional Content (per serving):

Cal |112Fat |8.3g Protein |9g   Carbs| 16g Fibre| 1.5 g

Ingredients:

- ❖ 1 block of firm tofu
- ❖ 100 grams (1/2 cup) of all-purpose flour
- ❖ 15 grams (1 tablespoon) of cornstarch
- ❖ 8 grams (1 teaspoon) of paprika

- ❖ 1 grain (1 pinch) of salt
- ❖ 1 grain (1 pinch) of ground black pepper
- ❖ 60 ml (1/4 cup) of water

Directions:

1. Cut the tofu into small cubes.
2. In a bowl, combine the flour, cornstarch, paprika, salt and black pepper.
3. Add the water and mix until you get a smooth paste.
4. Dip each cube of tofu in the batter and coat well.
5. Place the coated tofu cubes on a baking sheet lined with parchment paper.
6. Preheat the Air fryer to 200°C (400°F).
7. Place the baking sheet with the tofu nuggets in the air fryer basket and Air fry for about 10-12 minutes, until golden brown and crispy.
8. Remove the tofu nuggets from the air fryer and serve hot with a sauce of your choice.
9. Enjoy your snack!

72. VEGAN AIR FRYER ZUCCHINI CHIPS

Servings|3Time|10 minutes

Nutritional Content (per serving):

Cal |102Fat |6g Protein |5.3g   Carbs| 13g Fibre| 1.4 g

Ingredients:

- ❖ 2 medium zucchini, 200 grams (1/2 pound)
- ❖ 100 grams (1/2 cup) of all-purpose flour
- ❖ 100 grams (1/2 cup) of almond milk
- ❖ 100 grams (1/2 cup) of panko breadcrumbs

- ❖ grain (1 pinch) of salt
- ❖ 1 grain (1 pinch) of ground black pepper
- ❖ 15 grams (1 tablespoon) of Italian seasoning (or a spice blend of your choice)

Directions:

1. Preheat the Air fryer to 190° C (380°F)
2. Wash the zucchini and cut them into thin slices.
3. In a bowl, mix the flour and the almond milk to form a smooth paste.
4. In another bowl, combine the panko breadcrumbs, Italian seasoning, salt and black pepper.
5. Dip each slice of zucchini in the flour and milk-based batter, and then coat them with panko breadcrumbs.
6. Place the coated zucchini rounds on a baking sheet lined with parchment paper.
7. Place the baking sheet with the zucchini rounds in the air fryer and cook for about 8 to 10 minutes, until golden brown and crispy.
8. Remove the zucchini chips from the air fryer and serve hot with a sauce of your choice.
9. Serve and enjoy your zucchini chips!

73. VEGAN AIR FRYER POTATO FRIES

Servings|3-4Time|20 minutes

Nutritional Content (per serving):

Cal |110Fat |7g Protein |4.8g   Carbs| 12g Fibre| 1.3 g

Ingredients:

- ❖ 4 medium potatoes, 750 grams (1 ½ pounds)
- ❖ 15 ml (1 heap tablespoon) of vegetable or olive oil
- ❖ 8 grams (1 teaspoon) of paprika
- ❖ 4 grams (1/2 teaspoon) ground cumin
- ❖ 1 grain (1 pinch) of salt
- ❖ 1 grain (1 pinch) of ground black pepper
- ❖ 4 grams (1/2 teaspoon) of garlic powder

Directions:

1. Start by washing the potatoes and cutting them into sticks.
2. In a bowl, combine the olive oil, paprika, ground cumin, garlic powder, salt, and black pepper.
3. Add the potato sticks to the bowl and stir until well coated in the spicy marinade.
4. Put the potato sticks on a baking sheet lined with parchment paper.
5. Preheat the Air fryer to 200° C (400°F).
6. Place the baking sheet with the potato fries in the air fryer and bake for 18 to 20 minutes, flipping halfway through, until golden brown and crispy.
7. Remove the potato fries from the air fryer and serve hot with a sauce of your choice.
8. Enjoy your potato fries!

74. VEGAN AIR FRYER CABBAGE CHIPS

Servings|3-4Time|20 minutes

Nutritional Content (per serving):

Cal |86Fat |4.6g Protein |4g   Carbs| 11g Fibre| 1.5 g

Ingredients:

- ½ Head of cabbage; about 400 grams (1/2 pound)
- 15 ml (1 heap tablespoon) of olive oil

- 1 grain (1 pinch) of salt
- 1 grain (1 pinch) of ground black pepper

Directions:

1. Preheat your air fryer to 150° C (300°F).
2. Separate the cabbage papers each from the other, you can chop them to your liking in terms of size; then wash the cabbage leaves and dry them thoroughly with paper towel.
3. In a large and deep bowl, combine the olive oil, with the salt and the ground black pepper.
4. Add the cabbage pieces to the bowl and toss until well coated in the oil and spices.
5. Place the coated cabbage pieces on a baking sheet lined with parchment paper.
6. Place the baking sheet with the cabbage chips in the air fryer and bake for 8-10 minutes, until golden brown and crispy.
7. Remove the cabbage chips from the air fryer and serve hot with a sauce of your choice.
8. Enjoy your cabbage chips!

75. VEGAN AIR FRYER OKRA

Servings|3-4Time|20 minutes

Nutritional Content (per serving):

Cal |110Fat |7g Protein |4.8g   Carbs| 12g Fibre| 1.3 g

Ingredients:

- ❖ 450grams (1 pound) of okra;
- ❖ 100 grams (1/2 cup) of rice flour;
- ❖ 50 grams (1/4 cup) of semolina or flour
- ❖ 15 grams (1 tablespoon) of nigella seeds;

- ❖ 4 grams (1/2 teaspoon) of fennel seeds;
- ❖ 4 grams (1/2 teaspoon) of turmeric powder;
- ❖ 4 grams (1/2 teaspoon) of chili pepper powder,
- ❖ 250 ml (1 cup) of water.
- ❖ 15 ml (1 heap tablespoon) of vegetable oil
- ❖ Lemon slices
- ❖ 1 grain (1 pinch) of salt
- ❖ 1 grain (1 pinch) of ground black pepper

Directions:

1. Wash the okras and dry them with a paper towel.
2. Cut the okra vertically. Stir in flour, rice and wheat semolina, fennel and nigella seeds, turmeric, black pepper powder and salt to taste. Mix well; then add the water and the point of the paste is thick.
3. Rinse the okra in the batter; it covers all the pieces well. Let it sit for about 15 minutes.
4. Cover the okra with a little olive oil and place them in the basket of your Air Fryer, airing as best you can. If it is necessary to air-fry in more than one batch
5. Cook for 10 minutes at 170° C (340°F); shake the okras, and turn to them, and then back to cook for 2 to 5 minutes, until they are crispy.
6. Serve immediately with lemon wedges.

76. VEGAN AIR FRYER ONION RINGS

Servings|2Time|10 minutes

Nutritional Content (per serving):

Cal |315Fat |7.6g Protein |3.6g   Carbs| 15g Fibre| 1.8 g

Ingredients:

- 1 large, sweet onion
- 100 grams (1/2 cup) of flour
- 1 egg
- 15 ml (1 tablespoon) of water
- 250 grams (1 1/2 cups) of panko breadcrumbs
- 4 grams (1 teaspoon) of onion powder

- 4 grams (1 teaspoon) of paprika
- 15 ml (1 tablespoon) of maple syrup
- 1 grain (1 pinch) salt
- 1 grain (1 pinch) of ground black pepper

Directions:

1. Cut the onion into 1/2-inch (1 cm) thick slices; then separate the slices into rings. Reserve the large slices in a bowl of fresh water (keep the smaller ones for another use).
2. Put the flour in a bowl. In another bowl, mix the egg and water. In a third bowl, combine the breadcrumbs, onion powder and paprika.
3. Season with salt and pepper; then dip the reserved onion rings in the flour, then dip them in the egg.
4. Repeat, dipping the slices again in the flour and then in the egg.
5. Finally, pass the slices in the breadcrumbs, turning them over and pressing lightly to coat them well.
6. Spray the basket of an air fryer with cooking spray. Place half of the onion rings in the fryer basket, in a single layer, and spray lightly with cooking spray.
7. Air fry at 375° F (180° C) for 10 minutes or until the slices are golden brown (turn them halfway through cooking).
8. Cook the rest of the onion rings in the same way. Let the rings rest for a few minutes.
9. Serve and enjoy your onion rings.

77.   VEGAN AIR FRYER AVOCADO FRIES

Servings|2Time|10 minutes

Nutritional Content (per serving):

Cal |213Fat |3g Protein |3.8g   Carbs| 13g Fibre| 1.5 g

Ingredients:

- ❖ 2-4 ripe avocados
- ❖ 100 grams (1/2 cup) of all use flour
- ❖ 100 grams (½ cup) of Panko breadcrumbs
- ❖ 2 grams (1/4 teaspoon of) paprika
- ❖ 15 grams (1 tablespoon) of cornstarch

- ❖ 1 tablespoon of nutritional yeast
- ❖ 3/4 cup of unsweetened almond milk
- ❖ 15 ml (1 tablespoon) of apple cider vinegar
- ❖ 15 ml (1 heap tablespoon) of cooking oil
- ❖ 1 grain (1 pinch) salt
- ❖ 1 grain (1 pinch) of ground black pepper

Directions:

1. Preheat your Air fryer at 200 ° C (400°F)
2. Cut the avocados into slices about 1 cm thick.
3. In a bowl, mix the flour, salt, pepper and paprika.
4. In another bowl, mix the cornstarch, nutritional yeast, almond milk and apple cider vinegar to form a thick paste.
5. Dip each slice of avocado in the flour, then in the dough based on almond milk, then in the Panko breadcrumbs to coat well.
6. Lightly spray the avocado slices coated with aerosol cooking oil.
7. Place the avocado slices in the basket of the Air fryer.
8. Cook for 8 to 10 minutes or until avocado fries are golden and crisp.
9. Serve and enjoy your avocado fries!

78. VEGAN AIR FRYER GARLICKY POTATO NUGGETS

Servings|2Time|25 minutes

Nutritional Content (per serving):

Cal |250Fat |4.5g Protein |3.1g   Carbs| 12g Fibre| 1.9 g

Ingredients:

- ❖ 3 to 4; 450 grams (1 pound) of medium sized potatoes
- ❖ 30 ml (2 tablespoons) of olive oil
- ❖ 2 grams (1/4 teaspoon) of garlic powder
- ❖ 1 grain (1 pinch) salt
- ❖ 1 grain (1 pinch) of ground black pepper
- ❖ 2 grams (1/4 teaspoon) of smoked paprika

Directions:

1. Preheat your air fryer at 200 ° C (400°F).
2. Wash and peel the potatoes. Cut them into square or rectangular pieces, about 2 cm long and wide.
3. In a bowl, mix the olive oil, salt, pepper, powdered garlic and smoked paprika.
4. Add the potato pieces to the oil and spices mixture and mix well to coat them.
5. Place the potato pieces in the basket of the air fryer.
6. Cook for about 15 to 20 minutes, shaking the basket every 5 minutes so that the potato nuggets cook evenly.
7. Serve the nuggets of hot potatoes with a sauce of your choice, such as vegan mayonnaise, ketchup or a vegan barbecue sauce.

79.   VEGAN AIR FRYER CARROTS FRIES

Servings|4Time|25 minutes

Nutritional Content (per serving):

Cal |180Fat |5.6g Protein |4.8g   Carbs| 15g Fibre| 2 g

Ingredients:

- ❖ 7 medium carrots 450 grams (1 pound)
- ❖ 15 ml (1 heap tablespoon) of olive oil
- ❖ 2 grams (1/4 teaspoon) of paprika teaspoon
- ❖ 2 grams (1/4) teaspoon of cumin

- ❖ 1 grain (1 pinch) salt
- ❖ 1 grain (1 pinch) of ground black pepper
- ❖ 2 grams (1/4 teaspoon) of smoked paprika

Directions:

1. Preheat your Air fryer at 200 ° C (400°F)
2. Wash and peel the carrots. Cut them into rectangular or square sticks, about 2 cm long and wide.
3. In a bowl, mix the olive oil, salt, pepper, paprika and cumin.
4. Add the carrot sticks to the oil and spices mixture and mix well to coat them.
5. Place the carrot sticks in the basket of your air fryer.
6. Cook for about 15 to 20 minutes, shaking the basket every 5 minutes so that the carrots are cooking evenly. Carrots must be golden and crisp.
7. Serve the hot carrots with a sauce of your choice, such as vegan mayonnaise, ketchup, or a vegan barbecue sauce.
8. Enjoy your air fried carrots.

80. VEGAN AIR FRYER CASSAVA ROOT FRIES

Servings|2 Time|20 minutes

Nutritional Content (per serving):

Cal |83 Fat |3.6g Protein |3.5g Carbs| 12g Fibre| 1.5 g

Ingredients:

- ❖ 2 cassava roots
- ❖ 15 ml (1 heap tablespoon) of vegetable olive oil
- ❖ 2 grams (1/4 teaspoon) of garlic powder
- ❖ 1 grain (1 pinch) salt
- ❖ 1 grain (1 pinch) of ground black pepper
- ❖ 2 grams (1/4 teaspoon) of smoked paprika

Directions:

1. Preheat your air fryer at 200 ° C (400°F).
2. Wash and peel the cassava roots. Cut them into fine round slices, using a mandolin or a knife.
3. In a bowl, mix the olive oil, salt, pepper, and garlic powder.
4. Add the cassava slices to the oil and spices mixture and mix well to coat them.
5. Place the cassava slices in the basket of your air fryer.
6. Cook for about 10 to 15 minutes, shaking the basket every 5 minutes so that the cassava chips cook evenly.
7. Remove the cassava chips from your air fryer and let them cool for a few minutes before serving.

81. VEGAN AIR FRYER QUINOA STUFFED PEPPERS

Servings|4Time|20 minutes

Nutritional Content (per serving):

Cal |125Fat |6g Protein |4g   Carbs| 13g Fibre| 1.7 g

Ingredients:

- ❖ 4 red peppers
- ❖ 1 cup (200 grams) of cooked quinoa
- ❖ 100 grams (1/2 cup) of shredded vegan cheese
- ❖ 100 grams (1/2 cup) of chopped fresh parsley

- ❖ 1 grain (1 pinch) salt
- ❖ 1 grain (1 pinch) of ground black pepper
- ❖ 30 ml (2 heap tablespoons) of olive oil
- ❖ 50 grams (1/4 cup) of chopped red onion
- ❖ 1 minced garlic clove

Directions:

1. Preheat your air fryer to a temperature of about 200° C (400°F).
2. Cut the peppers in half lengthwise and remove the seeds and white membranes.
3. In a bowl, combine all together the cooked quinoa with the grated vegan cheese, the chopped fresh parsley, the chopped red onion, the chopped garlic, the salt and black pepper.
4. Fill each of the pepper halves with the quinoa and the vegan cheese mixture.
5. Place the stuffed peppers in your air fryer and drizzle with olive oil.
6. Bake your peppers for about 15 to 20 minutes, until they become golden and crispy.
7. Serve your rolled peppers hot, garnished with fresh parsley if desired.
8. Enjoy your stuffed peppers!

82. VEGAN AIR FRYER VEGAN PIZZA

Servings|4Time|12 minutes

Nutritional Content (per serving):

Cal |150Fat |7g Protein |7g   Carbs| 12.2g Fibre| 1.8 g

Ingredients:

- 1 ball of vegan pizza dough, about ½ pound (250 grams)
- 100 ml (1/2 cup) of tomato sauce
- 200 grams (1 cup) of fresh broccoli cut into small pieces
- 50 grams (1/4 cup) of red onion cut into small pieces
- 50 grams (1/4 cup) of red bell pepper cut into small pieces
- 100 grams (1/2 cup) of shredded vegan cheese
- 15 ml (1 heap tablespoon) of vegetable or olive oil
- 1 grain (1 pinch) salt
- 1 grain (1 pinch) of ground black pepper

Directions:

1. Preheat your Air fryer to 200°C (400°F).
2. Roll out your pizza dough on top of a lightly floured surface.
3. Spread the tomato sauce on the pizza dough, leaving a border of about 2 cm on the sides.
4. Scatter the broccoli, red onion, and red pepper pieces over the tomato sauce.
5. Sprinkle the shredded vegan cheese over the vegetables.
6. Drizzle your pizza with olive oil and season with salt and black pepper.
7. Place your pizza in the basket of your air fryer and cook for about 10-12 minutes, until the crust is golden brown and crispy, and the vegan cheese is melted.
8. Remove the pizza out of your air fryer and let it cool a little, then slice it and serve it hot.
9. Serve and enjoy your pizza!

83.   VEGAN AIR FRYER ROSTI

Servings|2-4Time|15 minutes

Nutritional Content (per serving):

Cal |230Fat |12g Protein |8g   Carbs| 13g Fibre| 2.3 g

Ingredients:

- 2 medium potatoes, peeled and grated 450 grams (1 pound)
- 1 small onion, finely chopped
- 20 grams (2 tablespoons) of flour
- 10 grams (1 tablespoon) of nutritional yeast
- 5 grams (1 teaspoon) of paprika
- 2.5grams (1/2 teaspoon) of garlic powder
- Salt and pepper, to taste
- Cooking spray or oil, for greasing

Directions:

1. Preheat your air fryer to a temperature of about 375° F (190° C).
2. In a large bowl, mix the grated potatoes, chopped onion, flour, nutritional yeast, paprika, garlic powder, salt, and pepper until well combined.
3. Divide your mixture into four portions; then shape each portion into a flat patty.
4. Spray or brush the air fryer basket with cooking spray or oil.
5. Place the patties in the air fryer basket, leaving some space in between.
6. Cook for about 12 to 15 minutes; making sure to flip halfway through, until the rosti are golden brown and crispy on both sides.
7. Serve hot and enjoy your Rosti!

84. VEGAN AIR FRYER BEET CHIPS

Servings|2Time|10 minutes

Nutritional Content (per serving):

Cal |85Fat 3g Protein |5g   Carbs| 10g Fibre| 2 g

Ingredients:

- ❖ 250 grams (1/2 pound) of peeled and thinly sliced medium beets
- ❖ 1 tablespoon olive oil
- ❖ 1 grain (1 pinch) salt
- ❖ 1 grain (1 pinch) of ground black pepper

Directions:

1. Start by preheating your air fryer to a temperature of about 190° C (380°F)
2. In a large deep bowl, toss all together the beet slices with the olive oil, the salt and the ground black pepper until it is very well coated.
3. Put the beet slices in your air fryer in one single layer, making sure the beet don't overlap.
4. Cook for about 10 minutes, until the chips become crispy and golden. If necessary, you can flip the chips halfway through the cooking process for even cooking.
5. Remove the chips from the air fryer and allow them to cool slightly before serving.
6. Enjoy your crispy and tasty beet chips!

85. VEGAN AIR FRYER CASHEWS

Servings|4 Time|7 minutes

Nutritional Content (per serving):

Cal |157 Fat 3g Protein |5g   Carbs| 8.6g Fibre| 0.9 g

Ingredients:

- ❖ 250 grams (1/2 pound) of unsalted cashews
- ❖ 15ml (1 heap tablespoon) of vegetable or olive oil or coconut oil
- ❖ 1 grain (1 pinch) salt
- ❖ 1 grain (1 pinch) of ground black pepper

Directions:

1. Preheat your air fryer to a temperature of about 190° C (380°F)
2. In a large deep bowl, toss the cashews with olive oil or coconut oil until well coated.
3. Place the cashews in the air fryer in a single layer.
4. Cook for about 5-7 minutes, stirring the cashews every few minutes to brown them evenly.
5. Remove the cashews from the air fryer and place them on paper towels to drain off excess oil.
6. Sprinkle with salt and ground black pepper, to taste; then toss the cashews to evenly coat.
7. Let cool slightly before serving.
8. Serve and enjoy your cashews!

WHOLE VEGAN AIR FRYER DESSERT RECIPES

86.   VEGAN AIR FRYER APRICOT PIE

Servings|4-6Time|30 minutes

Nutritional Content (per serving):

Cal |220Fat 4.6g Protein |6g   Carbs| 11g Fibre| 1.3 g

Ingredients:

Ingredients for the crust:

- ❖ 200 grams (1 cup) of all-purpose flour
- ❖ 60 ml (about 1/4 cup) of vegetable or coconut oil
- ❖ 60 ml (about 1/4 cup) of ice water
- ❖ 1 grain (1 pinch) of salt

Ingredients for the filling:

- ❖ 4 cups of halved and pitted fresh apricots
- ❖ 1/4 cup maple syrup
- ❖ 2 tablespoons cornstarch
- ❖ 1 tablespoon lemon juice
- ❖ 1 teaspoon vanilla extract

Directions:

1. Preheat your air fryer to a temperature of 190°C (380°F)
2. To prepare the crust, in a large bowl, combine the flour and salt. Add the coconut oil and mix until you get a sandy texture.
3. Add in the ice water and mix your ingredients until the dough comes together very well. Form a ball from your dough; then wrap it into a plastic wrap and refrigerate for a period of about 30 minutes.
4. To prepare the filling, in a separate bowl, combine the apricots, maple syrup, cornstarch, lemon juice and vanilla extract until the apricots are well coated.
5. Roll out the dough on a lightly floured work surface and transfer it to a pie pan. Prick with a fork.
6. Pour the filling of the apricot on top of the crust and spread it evenly.
7. Place the pie in the air fryer and bake for 25-30 minutes, or until the crust is golden brown and the filling is hot and bubbling.
8. Remove the pie from the air fryer and allow it to cool slightly before serving.
9. Serve and enjoy your Pie!

87. VEGAN AIR FRYER SUGAR-FREE VEGAN BROWNIES

Servings|4-6Time|30 minutes

Nutritional Content (per serving):

Cal |220Fat 4.6g Protein |6g   Carbs| 11g Fibre| 1.3 g

Ingredients:

- 200 grams (1 cup) of all-purpose flour
- 180 ml (3/4 cup) of maple syrup
- 80 ml (1/3 cup) of unsweetened cocoa powder
- 1 grain (1 pinch) of salt
- 4 grams (1/2 teaspoon) of baking powder

- 125 ml (1/2 heap cup) of unsweetened almond milk
- 125 ml (1/2 cup) of melted coconut oil
- 8 ml (1 teaspoon) of vanilla extract
- 100 grams (1/2 cup) of vegan chocolate chips

Directions:

1. Preheat your air fryer to a temperature of about 175° C (350°F)
2. In a large bowl, combine the flour, maple syrup, cocoa powder, salt, and baking powder.
3. Add in the vegetable milk, melted coconut oil and vanilla extract, and mix until all the ingredients are well incorporated.
4. Add the chocolate chips and mix gently.
5. Grease a brownie pan with coconut oil.
6. Pour your brownie batter into your prepared greased pan.
7. Place the brownie pan in the air fryer and bake for about 18-20 minutes.
8. Remove the brownie pan from your air fryer and let cool completely before cutting into squares.
9. Serve and enjoy your brownies!

88. VEGAN AIR FRYER SUGAR-FREE VEGAN WALNUT MUFFINS

Servings|6Time|20 minutes

Nutritional Content (per serving):

Cal |233Fat 6g Protein |11g   Carbs| 13g Fibre| 1.2 g

Ingredients:

- ❖ 200 grams (1 cup) of all-purpose flour
- ❖ 50 grams (1/4 cup) of almond flour
- ❖ 50 grams (1/4 cup) of coconut flour
- ❖ 30 grams (2 tablespoons) of baking powder
- ❖ 3 grams (1/2 teaspoon) of baking soda
- ❖ 1 grain (1 pinch) of salt
- ❖ 60 ml (1/4 cup) of melted coconut oil
- ❖ 250 ml (1 cup) of almond milk
- ❖ 15 ml (1 heap tablespoon) of apple cider vinegar
- ❖ 10 ml (1 teaspoon) of vanilla extract
- ❖ 100 grams (1/2 cup) of chopped walnuts

Directions:

1. Preheat your air fryer to a temperature of 180° C (360°F)
2. In a large deep bowl, combine all the flour together with the baking powder, the baking soda, and the salt.
3. In another deep large bowl, combine the melted coconut oil with the almond milk, the apple cider vinegar, and the vanilla extract.
4. Pour the liquid ingredients into the dry ingredients and mix until you get a smooth paste. Add in the chopped walnuts and mix very well again.
5. Pour the batter into silicone muffin cups, making sure to fill them 3/4 full. You can also use paper liners in your muffin tins.
6. Place the muffin cups in your air fryer basket and bake for about 15 to 20 minutes, or until the muffins are golden brown and a toothpick inserted in the center comes out clean.
7. Let muffins cool before serving.
8. Serve and enjoy your muffins.

89.   VEGAN AIR FRIED PEACHES

Servings|2Time|12 minutes

Nutritional Content (per serving):

Cal |208Fat 14g Protein |1.7g   Carbs| 21g Fibre| 2 g

Ingredients:

- 4 ripe peeled and quartered peaches
- 30 ml (2 heap tablespoons) of coconut oil
- 50 grams (1/4 cup) of almond flour

- 1 grain (1 pinch) of salt
- 50 grams (1/4 cup) of coconut flour
- 50 grams (1/4 cup) of rolled oats
- 30 grams (2 tablespoons) of maple syrup or stevia
- 8 grams (1 teaspoon) of ground cinnamon

Directions:

1. Preheat your air fryer to a temperature of about 200° C (400°F)
2. In a large deep bowl, combine all together the almond flour with the coconut flour, the rolled oats, the coconut sugar, the ground cinnamon and 1 pinch of salt.
3. Dip each of the peach wedges in the melted coconut oil; then in the flour mixture to coat.
4. Carefully arrange the coated peach wedges on the tray of your air fryer.
5. Bake the peaches for about 10-12 minutes, or until golden and tender.
6. Remove the peaches from the air fryer and serve warm, along with a scoop of vegan ice cream or vegan whipped cream, if desired.

90.   BANANA CAKE

Servings|4Time|35 minutes

Nutritional Content (per serving):

Cal |232Fat 12g Protein |6g   Carbs| 23g Fibre| 2 g

Ingredients:

- 3 ripe mashed bananas, about 750grams (1 ½ pounds), mashed
- 60 ml (1/4 cup) of apple sauce, it should be unsweetened
- 60 ml (1/4 cup) of vegan type of butter or of melted coconut oil
- 60 ml (1/4 cup) of milk, unsweetened

- 1 grain (1 pinch) of salt
- 15 ml (1 heap tablespoon) of apple cider vinegar
- 400 grams (1 pound) of all-purpose flour
- 125 ml (1/2 cup) of stevia or maple syrup
- 8 grams (about 2 teaspoons) of baking powder
- About 4 grams (1/2 teaspoon) of baking soda

Directions:

1. Preheat your hot air fryer to 160° C.
2. In a large bowl, combine the mashed bananas, applesauce, melted coconut oil, almond milk and apple cider vinegar.
3. In another bowl, combine the all-purpose flour, coconut sugar, baking powder, baking soda, and salt.
4. Stir the dry mixture into the banana mixture, stirring until the batter is smooth.
5. Pour your obtained batter into a previously greased cake tin.
6. Place the cake pan in the air fryer and bake for about 30 to 35 minutes, or until a toothpick inserted in the center of the cake comes out clean.
7. Remove the cake pan from the air fryer and let cool before serving.
8. Serve and enjoy your dessert!

91. VEGAN AIR FRIED OREO

Servings|4-6Time|5 minutes

Nutritional Content (per serving):

Cal |138Fat 11g Protein |8.3g   Carbs| 28g Fibre| 0.8 g

Ingredients:

- 200 grams (1 heap cup) of all-purpose flour
- 50 grams (1/4 cup) of cocoa powder
- 8 grams (2 heap teaspoons) of baking powder
- 50 grams (about 1/4 cup) of granulated monk fruit or maple syrup

- 1 grain (1 pinch) of salt
- 60 ml (1/4 cup) of unsweetened applesauce
- 60 (about 1/4 cup) of unsweetened almond milk
- 8ml (1 teaspoon) of vanilla extract
- 10-12 Oreo cookies (make sure they are vegan)

Directions:

1. Preheat your air fryer to 180° C (360° F).
2. In a mixing bowl, whisk together the flour, cocoa powder, baking powder, salt, and sweetener.
3. Add the applesauce, almond milk, and vanilla extract to the mixing bowl, and stir until you have a smooth batter.
4. Dunk each Oreo cookie into the batter, making sure it's coated evenly.
5. Place the battered Oreos in the air fryer basket, leaving space between each one so they cook evenly.
6. Air fry for 4-5 minutes or until the batter has crisped up and the Oreos are heated through.
7. Serve immediately and enjoy!

92. VEGAN AIR FRIED DONUTS

Servings|6Time|10 minutes

Nutritional Content (per serving):

Cal |120Fat 12g Protein |5g   Carbs| 18g Fibre| 0.8 g

Ingredients:

- 200 grams (1 heap cup) of all-purpose flour
- 50 grams (1/4 cup) of cocoa powder
- 8 grams (2 heap teaspoons) of baking powder
- 50 grams (about 1/4 cup) of granulated monk fruit or maple syrup

- 1 grain (1 pinch) of salt
- 60 ml (About 1/4 cup) of unsweetened applesauce
- 60 (about 1/4 cup) of unsweetened almond milk
- 8ml (1 teaspoon) of vanilla extract
- 10-12 Oreo cookies (make sure they are vegan)

Directions:

1. Weigh in your container (bowl or salad bowl) your fresh yeast first, to avoid any contact with sugar and salt which reduce its effectiveness, then place the flour on top.
2. Then add the sugar and salt, but do not work the dough right away.
3. Heat the milk, margarine, vanilla flavoring, and let cool.
4. Pour into your bowl or mixer bowl (fitted with the hook) and knead for about ten minutes, until you obtain dough that no longer sticks and is very flexible.
5. Cover your bowl with the help of a clean cloth and let your dough rise. Preferably, place the container in a warm place, or in the closed oven, to protect it from rafts.
6. Once the first growth is finished, remove the air from the dough to degas it (that's what we say in the jargon), and roll out the dough to about 2 cm thick.
7. Form the donuts using either an individual circle or a wide glass to make the marks and a knife.
8. Put the donuts on a baking sheet and make a second rise so that they take a little volume. This second growth is faster than the first; the goal is not for them to completely double in size, but to swell a little.
9. When your donuts are getting better, heat your air fryer to a temperature of about 200 °C (400°F)
10. Gently arrange the donuts in the basket of your Air Fryer and cook them for about 10 minutes on each side, making sure to shake once.
11. Serve and enjoy your donuts!

93. VEGAN AIR FRIED COOKIES

Servings|4Time|15 minutes

Nutritional Content (per serving):

Cal |115Fat 9g Protein |3.3g   Carbs| 19g Fibre| 0.9 g

Ingredients:

- 50 grams (about ¼ cup) of almond flour or almond flour
- 3/4 teaspoon (1.5 grams) of ground cinnamon
- 1/4 teaspoon (2 grams) of salt

- 2 medium ripe mashed bananas
- 100grams (1/2 cup) of almond butter or natural peanut butter
- 15 l (About 1 heap tablespoon) of vanilla extract
- 3/4 cup raisins or chopped dates

Directions:

1. Start by preheating your Air Fryer to a temperature of 180° C (360° F) Line a large baking sheet with a parchment paper or a silicone baking mat.
2. Whisk together oats, almond flour (or ground almonds), cinnamon and salt in a medium bowl.
3. Mash bananas, almond butter (or peanut butter) and vanilla together in a large bowl until creamy and well blended.
4. Add the dry ingredients and raisins (or dates) to the banana mixture and stir with a wooden spoon until everything is very well combined.
5. Scoop or roll level tablespoons of dough into balls and place on prepared baking sheet, making 12 cookies per batch.
6. Press down with a fork to flatten slightly.
7. Carefully place the baking sheet in the basket of your Air Fryer and cook for about 15 minutes.
8. Transfer the cookies to a wire rack to let them cool completely.
9. Serve and enjoy your cookies!

94. VEGAN AIR FRIED CARROT CAKE

Servings|4-5Time|35 minutes

Nutritional Content (per serving):

Cal |286Fat 12g Protein |6g   Carbs| 15g Fibre| 2.3 g

Ingredients:

- ❖ 400grams (1pound) of grated carrots
- ❖ 200 grams (1 heap cup) of all-purpose flour
- ❖ 200 grams (1 heap cup) of almond flour
- ❖ 8 grams (about1 heap teaspoon) of baking soda
- ❖ 4 grams (about 1 heap teaspoon) of baking powder
- ❖ 1 grain (1 pinch) of salt
- ❖ 8 grams (1 teaspoon) of ground cinnamon

- ❖ 4 grams (1/2 teaspoon) of ground nutmeg
- ❖ 125 ml (about 1/2 cup) of melted coconut oil
- ❖ 125 ml (about 1/2 cup) of unsweetened applesauce
- ❖ 125 ml (about 1/2 cup) of unsweetened almond-based milk
- ❖ 8 ml (1 teaspoon) of vanilla extract
- ❖ shredded coconut for garnish (optional)

Directions:

1. Start by preheating your air fryer to a temperature of about 180° C (360°F)
2. In a large deep bowl, combine all together the grated carrots with the all-purpose flour, the almond flour, the baking soda, the baking powder, salt, cinnamon and nutmeg.
3. In another deep bowl, combine the melted coconut oil with the applesauce, the almond milk and the vanilla extract.
4. Pour the wet ingredients into the dry ingredients and mix well until everything is incorporated.
5. Pour your obtained batter into a greased cake pan and bake in your preheated air fryer for about 30 to 35 minutes, or until a toothpick inserted in the center comes out clean.
6. Remove the cake from the air fryer and let it cool for a few minutes
7. Garnish with shredded coconut, if desired
8. Serve and enjoy your cake!

95. VEGAN AIR FRIED ALMOND BICUITS

Servings|6Time|12 minutes

Nutritional Content (per serving):

Cal |286Fat 11.3g Protein |6.3g Carbs| 18g Fibre| 2 g

Ingredients:

- ❖ 200 grams (about 1 heap cup) of almond flour
- ❖ 4 grams (about 1/2 teaspoon) of baking soda
- ❖ 1 grain (1 pinch) of tsp salt
- ❖ 60 ml (about 1/4 cup) of melted coconut oil
- ❖ 30 ml (2 heap tablespoons) of unsweetened applesauce
- ❖ 8 grams (about 1 heap teaspoon) of almond extract
- ❖ 200 grams (1 heap cup) of slivered almonds for garnish (optional)

Directions:

1. Start by preheating your air fryer to a temperature of about 180° C (360°F)
2. In a large and deep bowl, combine the almond flour with the baking soda and the salt.
3. In another deep bowl, combine the melted coconut oil, the applesauce, and the almond extract.
4. Pour the wet ingredients into the dry ingredients and mix well until everything is incorporated.
5. Form the dough into small balls the size of a golf ball and place them on a baking sheet lined with parchment paper.
6. Using a fork, press each ball of dough to flatten slightly and decorate them by sprinkling them with slivered almonds.
7. Place the baking sheet in the air fryer and bake the cookies for about 10-12 minutes, or until golden brown and slightly crispy.
8. Remove the cookies from the air fryer and let them cool completely before enjoying them.

96. VEGAN AIR FRIED CANNOLI

Servings|4Time|40 minutes

Nutritional Content (per serving):

Cal |325Fat 11g Protein |10.3g   Carbs| 25g Fibre| 1.6 g

Ingredients:

Ingredients for the dough:
- ❖ 200 grams (about 1 heap cup) of all-purpose flour
- ❖ 50 grams (about ¼ heap cup) of vegan margarine
- ❖ 60 ml (about 1/4 cup) of white wine
- ❖ 60 ml (about ¼ heap) cup of water
- ❖ 1 grain (1 pinch) of salt

Ingredients for the filling
- ❖ 400 grams (about 1 pound) of vegan cream cheese (cream cheese style)
- ❖ 60 ml (about 1/4 cup) of unsweetened almond milk
- ❖ 125 ml (about ½ heap cup) of unsweetened shredded coconut
- ❖ 10 ml (1 heap teaspoon) vanilla extract
- ❖ 50 grams (about 1/4 cup) of vegan dark chocolate chips (optional)
- ❖ Sugar- free sweetener to taste (optional)

Directions:

1. In a large bowl, combine flour and salt.
2. Add the margarine and work the dough until it is crumbly.
3. Add the wine and water and mix well until the batter is smooth.
4. Cover the dough and let it rest for about 30 minutes.
5. Meanwhile, prepare the filling by mixing the vegan cream cheese, almond milk, shredded coconut, vanilla extract, and sweetener (if desired) in a bowl until just combined and very well mixed.
6. Add in the dark chocolate chips, if desired.
7. Preheat your air fryer to a temperature of about 180° C (360°F)
8. Roll out the dough on a floured work surface until very thin (about 2mm thick).
9. Cut out circles of dough using a cookie cutter or a glass and wrap each circle around a heat-resistant metal tube (or cannoli's molds) previously oiled with oil of coconut.
10. Place the tubes in the air fryer and cook for about 5-7 minutes, or until the batter is golden brown and crispy.
11. Remove the tubes from the air fryer and allow them to cool slightly before removing the batter from the tubes.
12. Using a piping bag, fill each cannoli with the prepared filling.
13. Sprinkle with shredded coconut and dark chocolate chips, if desired.
14. Serve and enjoy your dessert!

97.   VEGAN AIR FRIED ORANGE CAKE

Servings|4Time|25 minutes

Nutritional Content (per serving):

Cal |235Fat 11g Protein |8.3g   Carbs| 12g Fibre| 1 g

Ingredients:

- 275 grams (1 1/2 heap cups) of all-purpose flour
- 15 grams (about 2 teaspoons) of baking powder
- 4 grams (1/2 teaspoon) of baking soda
- 1 grain (1 pinch) of salt
- 60 ml (about 1/4 cup) of melted coconut oil
- 125 ml (about 1/2 cup) of unsweetened almond milk
- 60 ml (about 1/4 cup) of freshly squeezed orange juice.
- 30 grams (2 heap tablespoons) of finely grated orange zest
- 10 ml (1 heap teaspoon) of vanilla extract
- 60 ml (1/4 heap cup) of agave syrup or maple syrup
- 30 grams (2 heap tablespoons) of ground flax seeds
- 60 ml (¼ cup, about 6 tablespoons) of water

Directions:

1. In a medium deep bowl, whisk all together the flour, with the baking powder, the baking soda, and the salt; and mix very well.
2. In another medium bowl, combine the melted coconut oil, unsweetened vegetable milk, freshly squeezed orange juice, finely grated orange zest, vanilla extract and agave syrup or syrup of maple.
3. In a small bowl, combine ground flax seeds and water. Let sit for 5 minutes, until the mixture becomes thick and gelatinous.
4. Add the flaxseed mixture to the liquid preparation and mix well.
5. Add the liquid mixture to the dry ingredients and mix until the batter is smooth.
6. Preheat the fryer to 180°C (360°F).
7. Pour your batter into the pre-greased cake pan.
8. Bake the cake for about 20 to 25 minutes, until golden brown and a toothpick inserted in the center comes out clean.
9. Let your cake cool for a few minutes before unmolding.
10. Serve and enjoy your dessert!

98. VEGAN AIR FRIED CHOCOLATE DIPPED DONUTS

Servings|6Time|20 minutes

Nutritional Content (per serving):

Cal |325Fat 11g Protein |10.3g   Carbs| 25g Fibre| 1.6 g

Ingredients:

For the donut dough:

- ❖ 450 grams (1 pound) of unbleached all-purpose flour
- ❖ 325 ml (1 ¼ cups) of almond milk at room temperature
- ❖ 10 grams (1 ½ teaspoons) of active dry yeast
- ❖ 60 ml of (1/4 cup) of stevia
- ❖ 100 grams (about ½ cup) of vegan butter
- ❖ 1 grain (1 pinch) of salt

For the chocolate icing

- ❖ 200 grams (about 1 cup) of vegan chocolate chips
- ❖ 125 ml (about ⅓ cup) of coconut oil
- ❖ 10ml (about 1 teaspoon) of maple syrup

Directions:

1. Whisk the milk, the yeast and 1 tbsp of the stevia together in a small bowl or measuring cup. Set your mixture aside for a period of about 10 minutes, until the mixture starts to become frothy.
2. In a medium bowl, using an electric mixer, beat altogether the butter and remaining sugar on high speed for 1 minute or until creamy. Then add the vanilla and salt.
3. Slowly add the yeast mixture, a small amount at a time, while mixing on low speed.
4. Add the flour by spoon to avoid splashing. Use a wooden spoon when the dough becomes too hard to mix with an electric mixer.
5. Keep adding flour until a soft ball of dough forms.
6. Transfer the dough to a lightly floured surface and knead for 5 minutes.
7. Put the dough in a bowl and place it in a warm place, with a damp kitchen towel over it, and let the dough rise for about an hour, until it doubles in size.
8. Punch the dough out and roll it out with a rolling pin on a floured surface until it is about ½ inch thick.
9. Use a cup or round shaped cookie cutter to make your donuts. For my part, I would rather use a drinking glass as well as a shot glass to make the holes in the donuts.

10. Transfer the donuts to parchment paper and cover them with a damp towel before placing them in a warm place for an hour to let them rise.
11. Preheat your air fryer to 180°C (350° F) (this will take about 3 minutes).
12. Put 2 donuts in the fryer basket and spray them with a little oil. Cook them for 5 minutes.

Make the chocolate icing:

13. In a bain-marie, melt all the ingredients and mix. As simple as that
14. Dip the cooked donuts in the mixture and put them on a wire rack for the glaze to set.
15. Serve and enjoy your donuts.

99. VEGAN AIR FRIED PUDDING

Servings|4Time|12 minutes

Nutritional Content (per serving):

Cal |260Fat 12g Protein |10.3g   Carbs| 18g Fibre| 1.3 g

Ingredients:

- 250 ml (1 cup) of almond milk
- 60 ml (about 1/4 cup) of coconut sugar
- 60 ml (about 1/4 cup) of all use flour
- 10 grams (1 heap tablespoon) of cornstarch
- 10 ml(1 heap teaspoon) of vanilla extract
- 4 grams (about 1/2 teaspoon) of ground cinnamon
- 1 grain (1 pinch) of salt
- 4 slices of vegan crumb bread cut into cubes
- 30ml (2 heap tablespoons) of fondue vegan margarine

Directions:

1. In a bowl, mix the almond milk, coconut sugar, all -use flour, cornstarch, vanilla extract, ground cinnamon and salt until the mixture is homogeneous.
2. Add the sliced bread cubes and coat them well with the mixture.
3. Lightly brush the basket of the hot air fryer with melted margarine.
4. Transfer the mixture of sandwich bread to the basket of the hot air fryer.
5. Cook at 180 ° C (360°F) for about 10 to 12 minutes until the pudding is golden and crisp.
6. Serve your dessert hot with vegan cream or a scoop of vegan ice cream.
7. Enjoy your dessert!

100. VEGAN AIR FRIED MONKEY BREAD

Servings|4-6Time|25 minutes

Nutritional Content (per serving):

Cal |276.3Fat 11.2g Protein |11.3g Carbs| 25g Fibre| 1.6 g

Ingredients:

- ❖ 2 ripe bananas
- ❖ 60 ml (about 1/4 cup) of almond milk
- ❖ 60 ml (about 1/4 cup) of melted coconut oil
- ❖ 15 ml (1 heap tablespoon) of apple cider vinegar
- ❖ 15 ml (about 1 tablespoon) of vanilla extract

- ❖ 400 grams (1 pound) of all use flour
- ❖ 60 ml of maple syrup (about 1/4 cup)
- ❖ 15 grams (about 1 tablespoon) of baking powder
- ❖ 4grams (about 1/2 teaspoon) of baking soda
- ❖ 1 grain (1 pinch) of salt

Directions:

1. Crush the bananas in a large bowl using a fork.
2. Add almond milk, melted coconut oil, apple cider vinegar and vanilla extract in the bowl with bananas. Mix well.
3. In another bowl, mix the all -use flour, maple syrup, baking powder, baking soda and salt.
4. Stir in the flour mixture in the banana mixture, stirring until the dough is well mixed.
5. Pour the banana bread dough into the basket of the hot air fryer previously greased.
6. Cook at 180 ° C (360°F) for about 20 to 25 minutes, until the bread is golden, and the top is firm to the touch
7. Remove the bread from the basket from the hot air fryer and let cool for a few minutes before serving.
8. Enjoy your Monkey bread!

101.   VEGAN AIR FRIED VEGAN MACAROONS

Servings|6Time|20 minutes

Nutritional Content (per serving):

Cal |215Fat 10.5g Protein |8.3g   Carbs| 13g Fibre| 1.4 g

Ingredients:

For the shells:

* 200 grams (1 heap cup) of almond flour
* 125 ml (about 1/2 cup) of non -sweet cocoa powder
* 60 ml (about 1/4 cup) of maple or agave syrup
* 60 ml (1/4 cup) of almond milk
* 10 ml (1 heap teaspoon) of vanilla extract

For garnish:

* 200 grams (1 heap cup) of cashews
* 60 ml (1/4 cup) of maple or agave syrup
* 10 ml (1/2 teaspoon) of vanilla extract
* 60 ml (about 1/4 cup) of water

Directions:

1. Preheat your air fryer at a temperature of about 160 ° C (320°F)
2. In a bowl, mix all together the almond flour and the cocoa powder.
3. Add the maple or agave syrup, almond milk and vanilla extract and mix well until the mixture is homogeneous.
4. Pour the mixture of shells into a pastry bag and make small circles of dough on a sheet of parchment paper.
5. Cook the shells at 160 ° C (360°F) for about 15 minutes.
6. During the cooking of the shells, prepare the filling. In a bowl, mix the cashew nut cream, maple or agave syrup, vanilla extract, and water until you get a homogeneous mixture.
7. Leave to cool the shells before garnishing them with the preparation with cashews.
8. Put the shells garnished in the air fryer for about 5 minutes to freeze the garnish.
9. Remove the macaroons from the hot air fryer and let them cool before tasting them.
10. Enjoy your macaroons!

Day 1:

Breakfast: Banana Cake

Lunch: Vegan Rice Balls with Sauce

Dinner: Spicy Tofu Salad

Day 2:

Breakfast: Vegan French Toast

Lunch: Vegan Samosa

Dinner: Sweet Potato Rolls

Day 3:

Breakfast: Vegan Cinnamon Oatmeal

Lunch: Eggplant Vegan Pasta

Dinner: Green Bean Salad

Day 4:

Breakfast: Leek and Mushroom Omelet

Lunch: Cauliflowers Tacos

Dinner: Rice with Beans

Day 5:

Breakfast: Tofu Scramble

Lunch: Vegan Mushroom Burgers

Dinner: Zucchini Gratin

Day 6:

Breakfast: Chickpeas and Shallots Bowl

Lunch: Potato Curry

Dinner: Bulgur Steaks

Day 7:

Breakfast: Vegan Polenta

Lunch: Spiced Chickpeas with Spinach

Dinner: Spicy Banana Chips

Day 8:

Breakfast: Breakfast Burritos

Lunch: Chickpea Falafel

Dinner: Beans & Sweet Potato Chili

Day 9:

Breakfast: Sugar Free Quinoa Breakfast

Lunch: Lentils with Edamame

Dinner: Air Fryer Beets

Day 10:

Breakfast: Blueberry Pancake

Lunch: Acorn Squash

Dinner: Avocado Rolls

Breakfast: Banana Cake

Lunch: Vegan Rice Balls with Sauce

Dinner: Spicy Tofu Salad

Day 12:

Breakfast: Leek and Mushroom Omelet

Lunch: Cauliflowers Tacos

Dinner: Zucchini Gratin

Day 13:

Breakfast: Avocado Pancakes

Lunch: Vegan Burgers

Dinner: Cabbage Fritters

Day 14:

Breakfast: Chickpeas and Shallots Bowl

Lunch: Potato Curry

Dinner: Black-Eyed Peas Curry

Day 15:

Breakfast: Sugar Free Quinoa Breakfast

Lunch: Lentils with Edamame

Dinner: Spicy Tofu Salad

Day 16:

Breakfast: Blueberry Muffins

Lunch: Green Veggies & Avocado Salad

Dinner: Tomato Caprese Salad

Day 17:

Breakfast: Vegan French Toast

Lunch: Kale and Potato Nuggets

Dinner: Sweet Potato Rolls

Day 18:

Breakfast: Air Fryer Bruschetta

Lunch: Lentil Burgers

Dinner: Cabbage Fritters

Day 19:

Breakfast: Vegan Frittata

Lunch: Lentil Meatballs

Dinner: Vegan Pizza

Day 20:

Breakfast: Banana Cake

Lunch: Vegan Rice Balls with Sauce

Dinner: Vegan Pulled Pork

Day 21:

Breakfast: Chickpeas and Shallots Bowl

Lunch: Potato Curry

Dinner: Air Fryer Okra

Thanks for Reading

We are grateful that you have chosen our Plant-Based Air Fryer Cookbook to help you on your journey towards a healthier and more sustainable lifestyle. We hope that our recipes have inspired you to try new plant-based dishes and have made it easier for you to incorporate more plant-based meals into your diet.

If you enjoyed using our cookbook, we would be grateful if you could leave a review. Your feedback helps us improve our cookbooks and helps others make an informed decision when choosing their next cookbook.

Thank you for your support and for being a part of our plant-based community. We can't wait to hear about your cooking adventures and see photos of your delicious creations.

Once again, thank you for choosing our Plant-Based Air Fryer Cookbook!

Printed in Great Britain
by Amazon